Crocheting
TEDDY BEARS
16 Designs for Toys

Barabara Jacksier
and
Ruth Jacksier

Dover Publications, Inc.
Mineola, New York

CONTENTS

INTRODUCTION 3

CROCHET INSTRUCTIONS 4

METRIC CONVERSION CHART 9

PANDA BEAR 10

SHAGGY BEAR 12

BRITISH BEAR 14

PINK and BLUE BEARS 16

KOALA BEAR 18

POLAR BEAR 20

BARNEY BEAR 22

GOLDILOCKS and THE THREE BEARS . . 24

PREPPY BEAR 28

HONEY BEAR 32

ROOSEVELT BEARS 35

Bibliographical Note

Crocheting Teddy Bears: 16 Designs for Toys is a new work, first published by
Dover Publications, Inc., in 1984.

International Standard Book Number

ISBN-13: 978-0-486-24639-0
ISBN-10: 0-486-24639-6

Manufactured in the United States by Courier Corporation
24639604
www.doverpublications.com

INTRODUCTION

As with most legends, the birth of the Teddy Bear is not documented by historic records. However, most bear historians maintain that it all began in 1902 with a much-publicized hunting incident involving Theodore Roosevelt and a small brown bear. While reports of the incident vary, historians relate that Roosevelt spared the life of the bear because of its wistful brown eyes.

A creative seamstress named Rose Michtom quickly stitched up two appealing stuffed bears to display in the window of her husband's small stationery shop. The response was overwhelming. Rose's plush bears sold out as fast as she could stitch them up! The Michtoms even sent the President one of their bears and asked his permission to call the original design a "Teddy" Bear in his honor. The President was delighted. The Michtoms became so successful in the stuffed-bear business that they gave up their Brooklyn, New York shop and founded the Ideal Toy Company.

America's most-loved stuffed toy has become synonymous with the trials and tribulations of growing up. And Teddy himself (or herself!) has grown up in the process. From that very first ginger-colored toy made in Brooklyn, the Teddy Bear family has branched out far and wide. Today's bear lover can choose from the wide-eyed Australian koala, roly-poly Chinese panda or the snowy white polar bear. Of course, the good old-fashioned Teddy Bear is still alive and well.

As you start to crochet your own Teddy Bears, hardly a day will go by without a new "inspiration." Sometimes it might be an intriguing yarn that just must be tried, or maybe a miniature hat (originally meant for a doll), or even an infant-sized T-shirt. Soon you'll have a collection of original Teddy Bears you can call your own.

Even two bears made from the same set of instructions will have their individual traits. Don't despair if an embroidered nose comes out a bit crooked or one ear tilts to the side . . . this may be Teddy's most endearing feature. When creating a bear for a special person or occasion, always keep those personal touches in mind: a graduation cap for the nursery-school valedictorian's bear or a tiny paint set for the amateur Van Gogh.

Those old enough to remember Teddy B and Teddy G, the famous characters from Seymour Eaton's series of illustrated books, *The Roosevelt Bears*, will surely appreciate a pair to call their own. Honey Bear, complete with her own honey hive, will delight children of all ages.

MATERIALS

Although most projects in the book recommend a specific brand of yarn so that you can duplicate the exact effect as pictured, we've also included a generic yarn name (fingering, sport, knitting worsted or bulky) in case you wish to substitute yarns. By choosing an equivalent-weight yarn you can make any (or every!) pattern resemble the bear of your dreams.

Most of our projects call for sew-on eyes. You can use whimsical movable types or realistic animal eyes made from glass or plastic. The lifelike eyes are generally available in sew-on, washer-secured or wire-tied types. To attach sew-on eyes, simply use a needle and thread. Washer-secured eyes must be inserted before the bear's head is stuffed. You push the eye through the crocheted piece from the right side, then push the washer on from the wrong side. These are very secure but have one disadvantage: it is not always possible to estimate the exact placement of features before the bear is stuffed. The washers are quite difficult to remove should you wish to move the eyes after the bear is completed. Many glass eyes are sold in pairs with a wire connecting the two. You will need a strong scissors or wire cutter to snip the eyes apart plus jewelry pliers to twist the wires into loops. These are then sewn on with needle and thread.

For noses, you can choose the sew-on plastic ones or embroider the traditional type using pearl cotton or embroidery floss. Both come in a large assortment of golds, browns and black. If you plan to make a bear for a very small child, you should embroider all features instead of using sew-on ones that might be pulled off and swallowed.

CROCHET INSTRUCTIONS

SLIP KNOT

Grasp the loose end of the yarn with your left hand and make an "O" with the yarn leading from the ball (the ball of yarn should be hanging behind the "O"). Pinch the top of the "O" between the thumb and middle finger of your left hand, and hold your crochet hook in your right hand as you would hold a pencil. Insert the tip of the hook and bring a loop from the yarn ball through the "O" (fig. 1). Tighten the loop to complete the slip knot (fig. 2). You are now ready to make your first chain stitch (remember that the loop on your hook never counts when you are counting the stitches in your work).

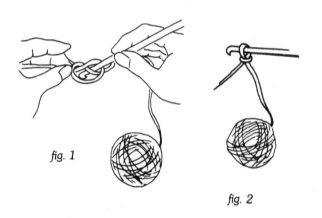

fig. 1

fig. 2

CHAIN STITCH

Pinch the base of the slip knot between the thumb and middle finger of your left hand, and wind the yarn from the ball from back to front over your forefinger. With the crochet hook inserted in the slip knot and the tip of the hook curved toward you, wrap the yarn around the hook from back to front (fig. 3)—this is called a yarn-over. Pull the yarn through the loop on the hook to complete the first chain stitch. Yarn-over again and pull through the loop on the hook the number of times specified (fig. 4). Each chain (and later each single crochet or other stitch) forms a distinct oval that can be clearly seen from the top of the work.

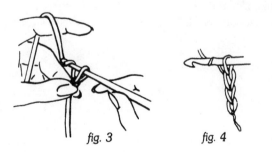

fig. 3

fig. 4

SINGLE CROCHET

Make a foundation chain of the required number of stitches (remember that the loop on the hook does not count as a stitch and that, for single crochet, you will need one chain for each stitch you want to make plus one additional chain for turning). Keeping the yarn from the ball wrapped from back to front over your left forefinger, begin the first single crochet stitch by inserting the hook from front to back in the second chain from the hook, taking care to push the hook through the center of the oval (fig. 5). Then yarn-over—that is, bring the yarn over the hook from back to front (fig. 6)—and pull the yarn through the stitch. You now have two loops on the hook (fig. 7). Yarn-over again (fig. 8) and pull the yarn through both loops on the hook to complete the first single crochet stitch (fig. 9). You now have only one loop left on the hook and are ready to begin the next stitch. Repeat the procedure until you have worked one single crochet stitch in each stitch of the foundation chain. Unless the pattern instructions specify otherwise, at the end of the first row and of each succeeding single crochet row, make one chain stitch (fig. 10) and then turn the work so the yarn from the ball is once again at the right edge. For succeeding rows of single crochet, unless the pattern instructions specifically tell you to do otherwise, always make the first stitch of a row in the last single crochet stitch of the previous row (that is, in the second stitch from the hook), not in the turning chain; and work each stitch by inserting the hook under both strands that form the oval of the stitch of the previous row (fig. 11).

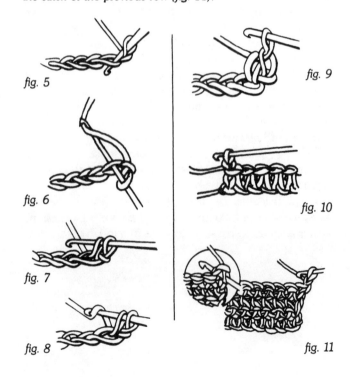

fig. 5

fig. 9

fig. 6

fig. 10

fig. 7

fig. 8

fig. 11

HALF DOUBLE CROCHET

Make a foundation chain of the required number of stitches (remember that the loop on the hook does not count as a stitch and that, for half double crochet, you will need one chain for each stitch you want to make plus two additional chains for turning). To begin the first half double crochet stitch, first make sure that the yarn from the ball is wrapped from back to front over your left forefinger. Then yarn-over (bring the yarn over the hook from back to front) and insert the hook from front to back in the third chain from the hook, taking care to push the hook through the center of the oval (fig. 12). Yarn-over again and pull the yarn through the stitch. You now have three loops on the hook (fig. 13). Yarn-over once more and pull the yarn through all three loops on the hook to complete the first half double crochet stitch (fig. 14). You now have only one loop left on the hook and are ready to begin the next stitch. Repeat the procedure until you have worked one half double crochet stitch in each stitch of the foundation chain. Unless the pattern instructions specify otherwise, at the end of the first row and of each succeeding half double crochet row, make two chain stitches and then turn the work so the yarn from the ball is once again at the right edge. For succeeding rows of half double crochet, unless the instructions specifically tell you to do otherwise, always make the first stitch of a row in the last half double crochet stitch of the previous row (that is, in the third stitch from the hook), not in the turning chain; and work each stitch by inserting the hook under both strands that form the oval of the stitch of the previous row.

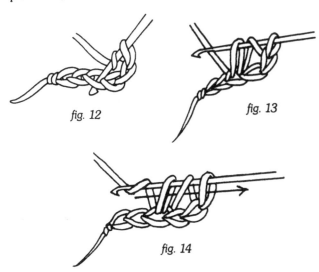

fig. 12   fig. 13

fig. 14

DOUBLE CROCHET

Make a foundation chain of the required number of stitches (remember that the loop on the hook does not count as a stitch and that, for double crochet, you will need one chain for each stitch you want to make plus three additional chains for turning). To begin the first double crochet stitch, first make sure that the yarn from the ball is wrapped from back to front over your left forefinger. Then yarn-over (bring the yarn over the hook from back to front) and insert the hook from front to back in the fourth chain from the hook, taking care to push the hook through the center of the oval (fig. 15). Yarn-over again and pull the yarn through the stitch. You now have three loops on the hook (fig. 16). Yarn-over again and pull the yarn through the first two loops on the hook. You now have two loops left on the hook (fig. 17). Yarn-over once more and pull the yarn through both

of the loops on the hook to complete the first double crochet stitch (fig. 18). You now have only one loop left on the hook and are ready to begin the next stitch. Repeat the procedure until you have worked one double crochet stitch in each stitch of the foundation chain. Unless the pattern instructions specify otherwise, at the end of the first row and of each succeeding double crochet row, make three chain stitches and then turn the work so the yarn from the ball is once again at the right edge. For succeeding rows of double crochet, unless the instructions specifically tell you to do otherwise, always make the first stitch of a row in the last double crochet stitch of the previous row (that is, in the fourth stitch from the hook), not in the turning chain; and work each stitch by inserting the hook under both strands that form the oval of the stitch of the previous row.

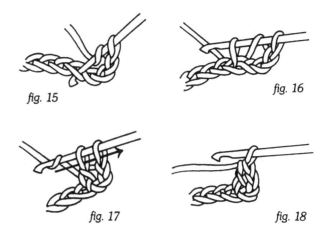

fig. 15   fig. 16

fig. 17   fig. 18

SLIP STITCH

Insert the hook in a stitch, yarn-over and then pull the yarn through both the stitch and the loop on the hook in one motion (fig. 19). Slip stitch is similar to single crochet, but you do not yarn-over a second time before pulling the yarn through the loop on the hook. It is an important utility stitch and is used, for example, to join the ends of a foundation chain to form a ring (fig. 20), to smoothly finish the edge of a piece worked in rounds and to work across an edge without adding appreciable height to the piece.

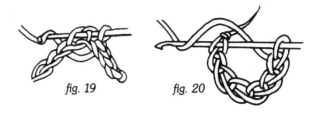

fig. 19   fig. 20

LOOP STITCH

This stitch is a decorative variation of single crochet, but it uses much more yarn and is always worked in patterns that alternate one row or round of loop stitch with at least one row or round of some other stitch—usually plain single crochet or half double crochet. Because the loops are formed on the back of the piece (the side facing away from you as you work), loop stitch is always worked from the wrong side so that the loops will appear on the right side of the finished piece. Thus, when working in rows, you will always work the loop stitch on the *wrong-side* rows and the other stitch of the pattern on the *right-side* rows. When working in rounds, the entire pattern is generally worked from the wrong side.

To practice the loop stitch, first make a foundation chain of the desired length and work one row of single crochet or half double crochet; then chain one stitch and turn the piece so the yarn from the ball is once again at the right edge. The next row will be worked in loop stitch. With the yarn from the ball wrapped from back to front over your left forefinger, begin the first loop stitch by inserting the hook under both strands of the second stitch from the hook as you would for single crochet (*see fig. 11*). To form the loop, swing the hook behind both of the strands on your forefinger (hold the finger close to the edge of the piece if you want a small loop and further away from the edge if you prefer a longer loop), catch the back strand with the tip of the hook (*fig. 21*), and then pull both strands through the stitch. You now have a loop around your forefinger and three loops on the hook (*fig. 22*). Yarn-over again (*fig. 23*) and pull the yarn through all three loops on the hook to complete the stitch (*fig. 24*). Tug the loop on your forefinger to tighten it and then remove your finger from the loop. You now have only one loop left on your hook and are ready to begin the next stitch. Repeat the procedure, taking care to make each loop the same length as the preceding one, until you have worked one loop stitch in each stitch across the row. Unless the pattern instructions specify otherwise, chain one stitch and turn the piece to the right side—you will now be able to see the finished loops of the row you have just completed (*fig. 25*); then work the next row in single crochet or half double crochet, as specified by the project directions. Continue in this manner, alternately working one loop stitch row and one single crochet or half double crochet row until you have completed the number of rows required.

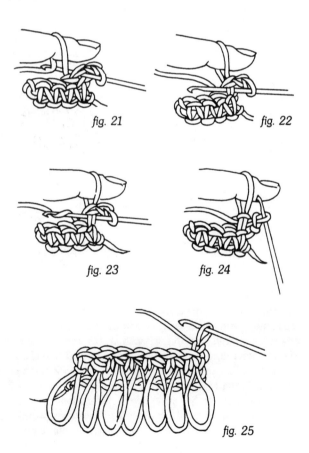

fig. 21   fig. 22

fig. 23   fig. 24

fig. 25

WORKING IN THE BACK LOOPS

When a *ribbed* effect is desired, the pattern instructions will tell you to work one or more rows or rounds in the back loops only. This means that, instead of inserting the hook in the customary way under both strands that form the oval of the stitch of the previous row or round, you must insert the hook under only the back strand (the one furthest from you) of the stitch (*fig. 26*).

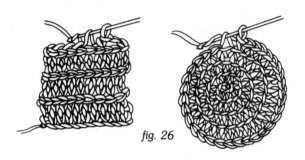

fig. 26

WORKING IN A CHAIN SPACE

A series of chain stitches is often used to bridge an open space—as, for example, when working a lacelike design. To crochet the next row, the pattern instructions may tell you to work across the "bridge" of chain stitches by working in the chain space rather than into the chain stitches themselves. This means that, to make each of the stitches in question, you must insert the hook into the space under the chain (*fig. 27*) and then work the stitch around the chain (*fig. 28*).

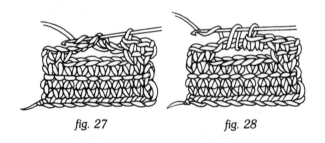

fig. 27   fig. 28

INCREASING AND DECREASING

To increase one stitch, work two stitches in the same stitch of the previous row; or work a stitch in the turning chain at the beginning or end of a row. Pattern instructions will specify which method to use.

To decrease one stitch, work two stitches together in the following way: work the first stitch until the final yarn-over, but do not yarn-over; instead, begin to work the next stitch, working it also to the final yarn-over; now yarn-over and pull the yarn through all loops on the hook.

ATTACHING NEW YARN

If you run out of yarn in the course of working a piece, complete a stitch with the old yarn; then hold the new yarn against the back of the work, leaving a loose 4-inch end. Insert the hook into the next stitch to be worked, yarn-over and draw a loop of the new yarn through the stitch. Then finish the stitch and continue working in the usual manner, using the new yarn. Hold the two yarn ends along the edge of the row and work them into the next few stitches or, if you prefer, let them hang at the back of the piece and weave them in later.

To change colors in the course of working a piece, work with the first color until you are ready to work the final yarn-over of the last stitch before you are to change colors. Then cut the first color, leaving a 4-inch yarn end. Now hold the new color against the back of the work, leaving a loose 4-inch end, yarn-over and pull a loop of the new color through all the loops on the hook to complete the stitch. Continue working in the usual manner, using the new color. Hold the yarn ends along the edge of the row and work them into the next few stitches or, if you prefer, let them hang at the back of the piece and weave them in later.

When you must attach new yarn along the edge of a completed piece in order to work an edging or the first row of another section of the project, hold the new yarn against the back of the work, leaving a 4-inch end. Insert the hook into the edge of the piece into the stitch in which the yarn is to be attached, yarn-over and draw a loop through the stitch; then chain one (that is, yarn-over again and draw through the loop on the hook). You are now ready to pick up and work the number of stitches specified in the project instructions. Hold the yarn end along the edge of the piece and work it into the first few stitches or, if you prefer, let it hang at the back of the piece and weave it in later.

ENDING OFF
Complete the last stitch of the piece and cut the yarn from the ball, leaving a 4-inch yarn end (or a yarn end of the length specified in the instructions). Then draw the yarn end through the remaining loop on the hook and pull tight. Thread the yarn end on a large-eyed yarn needle, weave it through the back of the work for about 1 inch, and trim the excess.

JOINING CROCHETED PIECES
Crocheted Seam: Pin or hold the pieces together (right or wrong sides out, as appropriate) and align the edges to be joined, matching stitches and rows as closely as possible. Hold your yarn at the back of the work, insert the hook from front to back through both loops of the first pair of matching stitches, yarn-over and pull a loop through to the front of the work. Insert the hook through both loops of the next pair of matching stitches, yarn-over and pull a loop through the stitches and the loop on the hook. Continue working in this manner, making a slip stitch

through both loops of each pair of matching stitches along the length of the edges being joined *(fig. 29)*. Crocheting through both loops will produce a ridge on the front of the work. For a flatter seam that has the appearance of parallel lines of stitches on the front of the work, slip stitch through only the inner loops of each pair of matching stitches *(fig. 30)*; or for a similar seam with the parallel lines on the reverse side of the work, slip stitch though the outer loops only *(fig. 31)*.

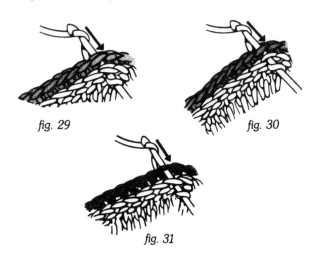

fig. 29   fig. 30

fig. 31

Sewn Seam: Pin or hold the pieces together as for a crocheted seam. Thread a large-eyed yarn needle with your yarn, and then work an overcast stitch through loops of each pair of matching stitches. Sew through the inner loops only if you want to produce parallel lines on the front of the work *(fig. 32)*; stitch through the outer loops only if you want the parallel lines to appear on the reverse side of the work *(fig. 33)*.

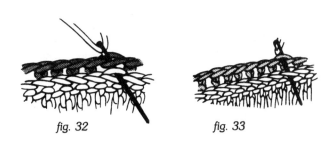

fig. 32   fig. 33

GENERAL INSTRUCTIONS

* (Asterisk) : This symbol indicates that the instructions immediately following are to be repeated the given number of times plus the original.

Repeat instructions in parentheses as many times as specified. For example: "(Ch 5, sc in next sc) 5 times" means to work all that is in parentheses 5 times in total.

Hook Conversion Chart

Aluminum

U.S. Size	B	C	D	E	F	G	H	I	J	K
British & Canadian Size	12	11	10	9	8	7	5	4	3	2
Metric Size	2½	3	—	3½	4	4½	5	5½	6	7

Steel

U.S. Size	00	0	1	2	3	4	5	6
British & Canadian Size	000	00	0	1	—	1½	2	2½

Stitch Conversion Chart

U.S. Name	Equivalent
Chain	Chain
Slip	Single crochet
Single crochet	Double crochet
Half double or short-double crochet	Half-treble crochet
Double crochet	Treble crochet
Treble crochet	Double-treble crochet
Double-treble crochet	Treble-treble crochet
Treble-treble or long-treble crochet	Quadruple-treble crochet
Afghan stitch	Tricot crochet

CROCHET ABBREVIATIONS

ch—chain
sc—single crochet
dc—double crochet
st, sts—stitch, stitches
sl st—slip stitch
rnd—round
yo—yarn-over

METRIC CONVERSION CHART

CONVERTING INCHES TO CENTIMETERS AND YARDS TO METERS

mm — millimeters   cm — centimeters   m — meters

INCHES INTO MILLIMETERS AND CENTIMETERS
(Slightly rounded off for convenience)

inches	mm		cm	inches	cm	inches	cm	inches	cm
1/8	3mm			5	12.5	21	53.5	38	96.5
1/4	6mm			5 1/2	14	22	56	39	99
3/8	10mm	or	1cm	6	15	23	58.5	40	101.5
1/2	13mm	or	1.3cm	7	18	24	61	41	104
5/8	15mm	or	1.5cm	8	20.5	25	63.5	42	106.5
3/4	20mm	or	2cm	9	23	26	66	43	109
7/8	22mm	or	2.2cm	10	25.5	27	68.5	44	112
1	25mm	or	2.5cm	11	28	28	71	45	114.5
1 1/4	32mm	or	3.2cm	12	30.5	29	73.5	46	117
1 1/2	38mm	or	3.8cm	13	33	30	76	47	119.5
1 3/4	45mm	or	4.5cm	14	35.5	31	79	48	122
2	50mm	or	5cm	15	38	32	81.5	49	124.5
2 1/2	65mm	or	6.5cm	16	40.5	33	84	50	127
3	75mm	or	7.5cm	17	43	34	86.5		
3 1/2	90mm	or	9cm	18	46	35	89		
4	100mm	or	10cm	19	48.5	36	91.5		
4 1/2	115mm	or	11.5cm	20	51	37	94		

YARDS TO METERS
(Slightly rounded off for convenience)

yards	meters	yards	meters	yards	meters	yards	meters	yards	meters
1/8	0.15	2 1/8	1.95	4 1/8	3.80	6 1/8	5.60	8 1/8	7.45
1/4	0.25	2 1/4	2.10	4 1/4	3.90	6 1/4	5.75	8 1/4	7.55
3/8	0.35	2 3/8	2.20	4 3/8	4.00	6 3/8	5.85	8 3/8	7.70
1/2	0.50	2 1/2	2.30	4 1/2	4.15	6 1/2	5.95	8 1/2	7.80
5/8	0.60	2 5/8	2.40	4 5/8	4.25	6 5/8	6.10	8 5/8	7.90
3/4	0.70	2 3/4	2.55	4 3/4	4.35	6 3/4	6.20	8 3/4	8.00
7/8	0.80	2 7/8	2.65	4 7/8	4.50	6 7/8	6.30	8 7/8	8.15
1	0.95	3	2.75	5	4.60	7	6.40	9	8.25
1 1/8	1.05	3 1/8	2.90	5 1/8	4.70	7 1/8	6.55	9 1/8	8.35
1 1/4	1.15	3 1/4	3.00	5 1/4	4.80	7 1/4	6.65	9 1/4	8.50
1 3/8	1.30	3 3/8	3.10	5 3/8	4.95	7 3/8	6.75	9 3/8	8.60
1 1/2	1.40	3 1/2	3.20	5 1/2	5.05	7 1/2	6.90	9 1/2	8.70
1 5/8	1.50	3 5/8	3.35	5 5/8	5.15	7 5/8	7.00	9 5/8	8.80
1 3/4	1.60	3 3/4	3.45	5 3/4	5.30	7 3/4	7.10	9 3/4	8.95
1 7/8	1.75	3 7/8	3.55	5 7/8	5.40	7 7/8	7.20	9 7/8	9.05
2	1.85	4	3.70	6	5.50	8	7.35	10	9.15

AVAILABLE FABRIC WIDTHS

25"	65cm	50"	127cm
27"	70cm	54"/56"	140cm
35"/36"	90cm	58"/60"	150cm
39"	100cm	68"/70"	175cm
44"/45"	115cm	72"	180cm
48"	122cm		

AVAILABLE ZIPPER LENGTHS

4"	10cm	10"	25cm	22"	55cm
5"	12cm	12"	30cm	24"	60cm
6"	15cm	14"	35cm	26"	65cm
7"	18cm	16"	40cm	28"	70cm
8"	20cm	18"	45cm	30"	75cm
9"	22cm	20"	50cm		

Shown in color on the front cover.

PANDA BEAR

SIZE: About 12″ high, sitting.

MATERIALS: Knitting worsted weight yarn, one (4 ounce) skein each of black and white; aluminum crochet hook size G; polyester fiberfill stuffing; tapestry needle; two 18mm animal eyes; red ribbon for bow; white glue.

GAUGE: 7 sc = 2″. To save time, take time to check gauge.

BODY: Starting at lower edge with white, ch 2.
Rnd 1: Work 7 sc in first ch made. Do not join rnds, use a marker. Move marker each rnd.
Rnd 2: * 2 sc in next sc. Repeat from * around (14 sc).
Rnd 3: * 2 sc in next sc, sc in next sc. Repeat from * around (21 sc).
Rnd 4: * Sc in each of next 2 sc, 2 sc in next sc. Repeat from * around (28 sc).
Rnd 5: * 2 sc in next sc, sc in each of next 3 sc. Repeat from * around (35 sc).
Rnd 6: * Sc in each of next 4 sc, 2 sc in next sc. Repeat from * around (42 sc).
Rnd 7: * Sc in each of next 5 sc, 2 sc in next sc. Repeat from * around (49 sc). Work even on 49 sc for 3″ more.
Decrease Rnd: Continue to work in sc, decreasing 7 sc evenly spaced around (42 sc).

Repeat decrease rnd 5 times more, stuffing body as you work. Break off leaving an 8″ end. Add more stuffing. Sew opening closed.

ARMS: Make 2. With black, ch 2.
Rnd 1: Work 7 sc in first ch made.
Rnd 2: 2 sc in each sc around (14 sc).
Rnd 3: * 2 sc in next sc, sc in next sc. Repeat from * around (21 sc). Work even on 21 sc for 6 rnds more. Ch 1, turn.
Short Row 1: Sc in each of next 10 sc. Ch 1, turn. Do not work on remaining sts.
Short Row 2: Decrease 1 sc over next 2 sc, sc in each sc to last 2 sc, decrease 1 sc over last 2 sc (8 sc).

Repeat last row until 4 sts remain. Break off. Stuff arms firmly and sew to body.

LEGS: Make 2. With black, ch 2. Work as for arms until Rnd 3 has been completed.

Rnd 4: * 2 sc in next sc, sc in each of next 2 sc.
Work even on 28 sc for 6 rnds more. Ch 1, turn. Work short rows same as for arms. Stuff legs firmly and sew to body.

HEAD: With white, ch 2. Work as for body until Rnd 7 has been completed.
Rnd 8: Sc in each sc around (49 sc).
Rnds 9 & 10: Continue to work in sc, increasing 7 sc evenly spaced around. At end of Rnd 10, join with sl st to first sc of rnd. Break off. Make another piece in same manner.

To join, sew or crochet both head pieces together, leaving an opening. Stuff head firmly, then sew opening closed. Sew head securely to body.

SNOUT: With white, ch 2. Work as for body until 4 rnds have been completed. Join and break off, leaving an 8″ end. Thread end into tapestry needle. Sew snout to head, stuffing lightly. With black yarn and tapestry needle, embroider nose in satin stitch and mouth in fly stitch.

EYE PATCHES: Make 2. With black, ch 7.
Row 1: Sc in 2nd ch from hook and in each remaining ch (6 sc). Ch 1, turn.
Rows 2 & 3: Sc in each sc. Ch 1, turn. At end of Row 3, do not ch-1. Break off, leaving an 8″ end. Sew eye patches to face as shown in photograph. Add eyes to center of each eye patch.

EARS: Make 4. With black, ch 10. Mark for lower edge.
Row 1: Sc in 2nd ch from hook and in each remaining ch (9 sc). Ch 1, turn.
Rows 2 & 3: Decrease 1 sc over first 2 sc, sc in each remaining sc across. Ch 1, turn.
Row 4: Decrease 1 sc at beginning and end of row. Ch 1, turn.
Rows 5 & 6: Decrease 1 sc at beginning of row, sc in each remaining sc. At end of Row 6, break off.

To join each ear, sew or crochet 2 pieces together, leaving lower edge open. Stuff lightly, then sew lower edges to head.

FINISHING: Tie ribbon around bear's neck and make a pretty bow.

Shown in color on the inside front cover.

SHAGGY BEAR

SIZE: About 14½″ tall, standing.

MATERIALS: *Unger's Gespa* (fringe-like bulky yarn), two (3½ ounce) skeins camel; aluminum crochet hook size P; polyester fiberfill stuffing; large-eyed tapestry needle; two 18mm sew-on animal eyes; green dotted or red satin ribbon 3″ wide, 1¼ yards; several yards of black mohair yarn for embroidering nose and mouth.

GAUGE: 1 st = 1″. To save time, take time to check gauge.

BODY: Starting at lower edge, ch 2.
Rnd 1: Work 7 sc in first ch made. Do not join rnds. Use a marker; move marker each rnd.
Rnd 2: Work 2 sc in each sc around (14 sc).
   Work even on 14 sc for 5½″ more. Stuff body firmly.
Decrease Rnd 1: Work 2 sts together 7 times. Break off. Leave top edge open for neck edge.

HEAD: Ch 2.
Rnd 1: Work 5 sc in first ch made.
Rnds 2 & 3: Work 2 sc in each sc around. Join with sl st. Break off.
   Make another piece in same manner. Using a length of matching yarn, sew or crochet both head pieces together leaving a small opening. Stuff firmly, then sew opening closed. Sew head securely to body.

SNOUT: Ch 2.
Rnd 1: Work 7 sc in first ch made.

Rnd 2: Sc in each sc around. Join with sl st to first sc of rnd. Break off leaving an 8″ end. Position on lower portion of head as shown in photograph; sew in place.

EARS: Make 2. Starting at lower edge, ch 3.
Rnd 1: Work 1 sc in 2nd ch from hook, sc in next ch. Break off. Sew to seam at top of head.

LEGS: Make 2. Starting at lower edge, ch 2.
Rnd 1: Work 6 sc in first ch made. Working in rnds, work even on 6 sc until leg measures 3½″ from beginning, turn.
Short Row 1: Sc in each of next 3 sc, turn.
Short Row 2: Sc in each of next 2 sc, turn.
Short Row 3: Sc in next sc. Break off. Stuff leg firmly and sew to body so the short rows extend up the side of the body.

ARMS: Make 2. Starting at lower edge, ch 2.
Rnd 1: Work 5 sc in first ch made. Working in rnds, work even on 5 sc until arm measures 3″ from beginning. Break off. Stuff and sew to body.

FINISHING: Sew eyes in place. With tapestry needle and black mohair yarn, embroider nose and mouth as shown in photograph: satin-stitch a triangular nose; work mouth in a fly stitch with a straight stitch at each end following pattern. Tie ribbon around bear's neck and make a pretty bow.

Shown in color on the inside back cover.

BRITISH BEAR

SIZE: About 14″ high, sitting.

MATERIALS: Knitting worsted weight yarn, 4 ounces of medium gray, 2 ounces each of light gray and black; aluminum crochet hook size G; polyester fiberfill stuffing; tapestry needle; fine sewing needle; black sewing thread; two ¾″ black buttons for eyes; small scraps of turquoise and white felt; white glue; a small piece of black suede (or felt) for elbow patches; four ⅝″ leather buttons; a piece of turquoise plaid ribbon for bow; a small pipe.

GAUGE: 7 sc = 2″. To save time, take time to check gauge.

BODY: With black, ch 2 for lower edge.
Rnd 1: Work 7 sc in first ch from hook. Do not join rnds. Use a marker; move marker each rnd.
Rnd 2: * 2 sc in next sc. Repeat from * around (14 sc).
Rnd 3: * 2 sc in next sc, sc in next sc. Repeat from * around (21 sc).
Rnds 4–6: Continue to work in sc, increasing 7 sc evenly spaced on each rnd.
Rnd 7: Sc in each sc around (42 sc).
Rnds 8 & 9: Continue to work in sc, increasing 7 sc evenly spaced on each rnd.
Work even on 56 sc for 2½″ more. At end of last rnd, join with sl st to first st of rnd. Break off black. Attach medium gray. Continue to work in sc, decreasing 7 sc on each of the next 6 rnds and stuffing body as you work. At end of last rnd, join with sl st to first st of rnd. Break off. Add more stuffing as needed.

HEAD: With light gray, ch 2. Work as for body until Rnd 9 is completed.
Rnd 10: Sc in each sc around. Join with sl st to first sc of rnd. Break off.
Make another piece in same manner.
To join, hold both head pieces together with right sides facing. Sew or crochet both pieces together, leaving an opening. Turn to right side. Stuff firmly, then sew opening closed. Sew head securely to body.

SNOUT: With light gray, ch 2. Work as for body until Rnd 3 has been completed.
Rnd 4: Sc in each sc around. Join with sl st. Break off, leaving an 8″ end. Thread end into tapestry needle and sew snout to center of one side of head, stuffing until firm.

EARS: Make 2. With light gray, ch 8 for lower edge.
Row 1: Sc in 2nd ch from hook and in each remaining ch (7 sc). Ch 1, turn.

Rows 2–4: Skip first sc, sc in each remaining sc. At end of Row 4, break off light gray. Attach medium gray and work a row of sc around shaped edge of ear. Break off. Sew ears to head.

LEGS: Make 2. With light gray, ch 2, for lower edge.
Rnd 1: Work 5 sc in first ch made. Do not join rnds.
Rnd 2: Work 2 sc in each sc around (10 sc).
Rnd 3: * 2 sc in next sc, sc in next sc. Repeat from * around (15 sc).
Rnds 4–6: Sc in each sc around. At end of Rnd 6, join with sl st to first sc of rnd. Break off light gray.
Rnd 7: Attach black, continue to work in sc, increasing 5 sc evenly spaced around.
Work even on 20 sc for 2½″ more. At end of last rnd, join with a sl st. Break off, leaving an 8″ end. Stuff legs and sew to body.

ARMS: Make 2. With light gray, ch 2 for lower edge, work as for legs until Rnd 3 has been completed.
Rnd 4: Continue to work in sc, increasing 5 sc evenly spaced around (20 sc). Join with sl st. Break off light gray.
Rnd 5: Attach medium gray, work even on 20 sc. Continue to work even on 20 sc until 13 rnds of medium gray have been completed. Ch 1, turn.
Short Row 1: Sc in each of next 9 sc. Do not work on remaining sc. Ch 1, turn.
Short Row 2: Skip first sc, sc in each of next 8 sc. Ch 1, turn.
Short Rows 3–6: Skip first sc, sc in each remaining sc. At end of Row 6, break off. Stuff arms and sew to body.

POCKET: With medium gray, ch 6 for lower edge.
Row 1: Sc in 2nd ch from hook and in each remaining ch (5 sc). Ch 1, turn.
Rows 2–4: Sc in each sc across. Ch 1, turn. At end of Row 4, do not ch 1. Break off. Attach black and work 1 rnd of sc around entire pocket. Join with sl st to first sc of rnd. Break off, leaving an 8″ end. Sew pocket to body, leaving top edge open.

ELBOW PATCHES: Cut 2 small ovals from black suede (or felt). With sewing needle and black sewing thread, sew elbow patches to arms as shown in photograph.

FINISHING: Sew buttons to chest. Using eye buttons for a pattern, cut 2 small half circles for eyelids. Glue one eyelid to top edge of each button. Cut 2 ovals from white felt for pupils. Glue below eyelids. Sew eyes to head. Tie ribbon around bear's neck and make a bow. With tapestry needle and black yarn, embroider nose in satin stitch. Place pipe in "mouth."

Shown in color on the front cover.

PINK AND BLUE BEARS

SIZE: About 9″ high, sitting.

MATERIALS: Knitting worsted weight yarn, one (3½ ounce) skein of pink or blue; 1 ounce of white; aluminum crochet hook size D and size G; polyester fiberfill stuffing; tapestry needle; two 12mm animal eyes for each bear; one ⅜″ animal nose for each bear; three white ½″-diameter pompons for each bear; white glue.

GAUGE: With size G hook: 7 sc = 2″; 7 sc rnds = 2″. To save time, take time to check gauge.

HEAD: Front: With pink or blue and size G hook, ch 2.
Rnd 1: Work 6 sc in first ch made. Do not join rnds. Use a marker and move marker each rnd throughout.
Rnd 2: Sc in first sc, 3 sc in next sc, sc in each of next 2 sc, 3 sc in next sc, sc in last sc (10 sc).
Rnd 3: Sc in each of next 2 sc, 3 sc in next sc, sc in each of next 4 sc, 3 sc in next sc, sc in each of next 2 sc (14 sc).
Rnd 4: * Sc in each of next 4 sc, 3 sc in next sc. Repeat from * once, sc in each of next 4 sc.
Rnd 5: Sc in each of next 6 sc, 3 sc in next sc, sc in each of next 4 sc, 3 sc in next sc, sc in each of next 6 sc.
Rnd 6: Sc in each of next 8 sc, 3 sc in next sc, sc in each of next 4 sc, 3 sc in next sc, sc in each of next 8 sc.
Rnd 7: Sc in each of next 9 sc, 3 sc in next sc, sc in each of next 6 sc, 3 sc in next sc, sc in each of next 9 sc.
Rnd 8: Sc in each of next 11 sc, 3 sc in next sc, sc in each of next 6 sc, 3 sc in next sc, sc in each of next 11 sc.
Rnd 9: Sc in each of next 13 sc, 3 sc in next sc, sc in each of next 6 sc, 3 sc in next sc, sc in each of next 13 sc (38 sc). Break off.
Back: Work as for head front for Rnd 1 (6 sc).
Rnd 2: * Sc in next sc, 3 sc in next sc. Repeat from * around (12 sc).
Rnd 3: * Sc in each of next 3 sc, 3 sc in next sc. Repeat from * around (18 sc).
Rnd 4: * Sc in each of next 5 sc, 3 sc in next sc. Repeat from * around (24 sc).
Rnd 5: * Sc in each of next 7 sc, 3 sc in next sc. Repeat from * around (30 sc).
Rnd 6: * Sc in each of next 9 sc, 3 sc in next sc. Repeat from * around (36 sc).
Rnd 7: * Sc in each of next 11 sc, 2 sc in next sc. Repeat from * around (39 sc). Break off.

SNOUT: With white and size D hook, ch 2.
Rnd 1: Work 6 sc in first ch made.
Rnd 2: * 2 sc in next sc. Repeat from * around (12 sc).
Rnd 3: Work 2 sc in each of next 8 sc, sc in each of next 4 sc (20 sc).
Rnd 4: Sc in each of next 6 sc, 2 sc in each of next 4 sc, sc in each of next 10 sc (24 sc).
Rnds 5 & 6: Sc in each sc around. At end of Rnd 6, break off, leave end of yarn for sewing.

To join, sew head back to head front, matching increased sections and leaving an opening at lower edge. Attach nose to snout (or embroider nose in satin stitch if desired); sew snout to head front, stuffing as you sew. Sew eyes to head front; stuff head firmly.

EARS: Make 2. With white and size D hook, ch 2.
Row 1: Work 5 sc in first ch made. Ch 1 turn.
Row 2: * 2 sc in next sc, sc in next sc. Repeat from * once, 2 sc in last sc. Ch 1, turn.
Row 3: Sc in each sc (8 sc). Ch 1, turn.
Row 4: 2 sc in first sc, sc in each of next 2 sc, 2 sc in each of next 2 sc, sc in each of next 2 sc, 2 sc in last sc. Break off white, join pink or blue. Ch 1, turn.
Row 5 (right side): With pink or blue, sc in each sc (12 sc). Break off. Sew ears to head.

BODY: Back: Right side is always facing you. With pink or blue and size G hook, ch 2.
Rnd 1: Work 6 sc in first ch made. Do not join rnds throughout.
Rnd 2: * 2 sc in next sc. Repeat from * around (12 sc).
Rnd 3: * Sc in next sc, 2 sc in next sc. Repeat from * around (18 sc).
Rnd 4: * 2 sc in next sc, sc in each of next 2 sc. Repeat from * around (24 sc).
Rnd 5: * Sc in each of next 3 sc, 2 sc in next sc. Repeat from * around (30 sc).
Rnd 6: Sc in each of next 2 sc, * 2 sc in next sc, sc in each of next 4 sc. Repeat from * around, end sc in each of last 2 sc (36 sc).
Rnd 7: * Sc in each of next 5 sc, 2 sc in next sc. Repeat from * around (42 sc).
Rnd 8: Sc in each of next 2 sc, * 2 sc in next sc, sc in each of next 6 sc. Repeat from * around. End sc in each of last 4 sc (48 sc).
Rnd 9: Sc in each sc around. Sl st in next sc. Break off.
Front: Work same as for back of body.

To join, sew both body pieces together with right sides facing and leaving an opening. Turn to right side; stuff firmly. Sew opening closed. Sew head securely to body.

ARMS: Make 2. Work as for back of body to end of Rnd 2. Working in sc, work even on 12 sc for 6 more rnds. Break off. Stuff firmly; sew last rnd to body.

LEGS: Make 2. With pink or blue and size G hook, ch 5.
Rnd 1: Work 3 sc in 2nd ch from hook, sc in each of next 2 ch, 3 sc in last ch. Working on opposite side of ch, sc in each of next 2 ch.
Rnd 2: 2 sc in each of next 3 sc (toe), sc in each of next 3 sc, 2 sc in next sc (heel), sc in each of next 3 sc. Join with sl st in first sc.
Rnd 3: Working in back loops only, sc in each sc around (14 sc).
Rnds 4–11: Working in both loops, sc in each sc around. At end of Rnd 11, sl st in next st. Break off. Stuff and sew in place.

FOOT PADS: Make 2. With white and size D hook, work as for legs to end of Rnd 2.
Rnd 3: Sc in each sc around (14 sc). Break off. Sew in place.

FINISHING: Sew or glue pompons to front of body as shown in photograph.

Shown in color on the inside back cover.

KOALA BEAR

SIZE: About 12″ high, sitting.

MATERIALS: *Pingouin's Super Chenille* (bulky weight chenille yarn), two (100 gram—3½ ounce) balls of tan and one ball of white; aluminum crochet hook size K; polyester fiberfill stuffing; tapestry needle; two 18mm sew-on animal eyes; koala-style black plastic nose; bow tie.

GAUGE: 4 sc = 2½″. To save time, take time to check gauge.

BODY: With tan, ch 2.
Rnd 1: Work 7 sc in first ch made. Do not join rnds. Use a marker, move marker each rnd. Work in back loops only throughout.
Rnd 2: * 2 sc in next sc. Repeat from * around (14 sc).
Rnd 3: * 2 sc in next sc, sc in next sc. Repeat from * around (21 sc).
Rnd 4: * Sc in each of next 2 sc, 2 sc in next sc. Repeat from * around (28 sc).
 Work even on 28 sc for 4″. Begin to stuff body as you work.
Decrease Rnd: Continue to work in sc, decreasing 7 sc evenly spaced around. Repeat decrease rnd, 3 times more, stuffing as you work. Join with sl st to first sc of rnd. Break off.

HEAD: With tan, work as for body until Rnd 4 is completed. Break off. Make another piece in same manner but do not break off. Hold both head pieces together with right sides facing. Leaving a 2″ opening, work around in sc, working through both thicknesses. Turn to right side. Stuff head firmly. Sew opening closed. Sew head securely to body.

EARS: Make 2. Starting at lower edge, with white, ch 7.
Row 1: Sc in 2nd ch from hook and in each remaining ch (6 sc). Ch 1, turn.
Row 2: Decrease 1 sc over first 2 sc, sc in each of next 2 sc, decrease 1 sc over last 2 sc. Break off. Sew straight edge of each ear to head as shown in photograph.

ARMS/LEGS: Make 4. With tan, ch 2.
Rnd 1: Work 7 sc in first ch made. Do not join rnds. Use a marker. Work in back loops only throughout.
Rnd 2: Sc around, increasing 5 sc evenly spaced around (12 sc).
Rnds 4—7: Sc in each sc around. At end of Rnd 7, join with sl st to first st of rnd. Break off. Stuff until firm, then sew arms and legs to body as shown in photograph.

FINISHING: Sew eyes and nose to face. Tie bow tie around neck.

Shown in color on the inside back cover.

20

POLAR BEAR

SIZE: About 13″ high, sitting.

MATERIALS: *Pingouin's Super Chenille* (bulky weight chenille yarn), two (100 gram—3½ ounce) balls of white; aluminum crochet hook size K; polyester fiberfill stuffing; tapestry needle; blue and white gingham ribbon 1″ wide, ½ yd.; two 16mm blue sew-on animal eyes; black plastic animal nose.

GAUGE: 4 sc = 2½″. To save time, take time to check gauge.

BODY: Ch 2.
Rnd 1: Work 7 sc in first ch made. Do not join rnds. Use a marker, move marker each rnd.
Rnd 2: Work 2 sc in each sc around (14 sc).
Rnd 3: * 2 sc in next sc, sc in next sc. Repeat from * around (21 sc). Work even on 21 sc for 5″ more. Stuff body firmly.
Decrease Rnd 1: Decrease 1 sc over next 2 sc, sc in next sc. Repeat from * around (14 sc).
Decrease Rnd 2: * Decrease 1 sc over next 2 sc. Repeat from * around (7 sc).
Decrease Rnd 3: (Decrease 1 sc over next 2 sc) 3 times. Break off, leaving a long yarn end. Thread end into tapestry needle and sew opening closed, adding more stuffing as necessary.

HEAD: Work as for body through Rnd 3.
Rnd 4: * Sc in each of next 2 sc, 2 sc in next sc. Repeat from * around. Break off. Make another piece in same manner. At end of rnd 4, join but do not break off.
  Hold both head pieces together with right sides facing. Leaving a 2″ opening, sc around edges, working through both thicknesses. Turn to right side. Stuff head firmly. Sew opening closed. Sew head securely to body.

EARS: Make 2. Ch 4 for top of ear.
Row 1: Sc in 2nd ch from hook and in each of the next 2 ch (3 sc). Ch 1, turn.
Row 2: 2 sc in first sc, sc in next sc, 2 sc in last sc (5 sc). Break off. Sew ears to head.

LEGS: Make 4. Ch 5 for top edge.
Row 1: Sc in 2nd ch from hook and in each remaining ch (4 sc). Ch 1, turn.
Rows 2–6: Sc in each sc across. Ch 1, turn. At end of Row 6, ch 3, turn.
Row 7: Sc in 2nd ch from hook, sc in next ch, sc in each sc across (6 sc). Ch 1, turn.
Row 8: Sc in each sc across. Break off. Join 2 pieces for each leg. Overcast pieces together from the right side. Stuff legs and sew to bear.

ARMS: Make 4. Ch 5 for top edge.
Row 1: Sc in 2nd ch from hook and in each remaining ch (4 sc). Ch 1, turn.
Rows 2–5: Sc in each sc. Ch 1, turn.
Row 6: 2 sc in first sc, sc in next sc, decrease 1 sc over last 2 sc. Ch 1, turn.
Row 7: Decrease 1 sc over first 2 sc, sc in next sc, 2 sc in last sc.
Row 8: Repeat Row 6.
  At end of Row 8, break off. Finish same as for legs. Sew arms to body.

FINISHING: Sew eyes and nose to face. Tie ribbon around neck and make a pretty bow. Cut a triangle out of each ribbon end as shown in photograph.

Shown in color on the front cover.

BARNEY BEAR

SIZE: About 19″ tall, standing.

MATERIALS: 8 ounces of medium brown knitting worsted weight yarn; aluminum crochet hook size G; polyester fiberfill stuffing; tapestry needle; two large movable eyes; 1 yard of yellow polka dot grosgrain ribbon 1½″ wide; 1″-wide piece of cardboard; several yards of black yarn for embroidering nose.

GAUGE: 7 loop sts = 2″. To save time, take time to check gauge.

TO WORK LOOP STITCH: When working loop stitch, wrong side of work is always facing you. Use cardboard as a guide or wind yarn around finger as desired. Insert hook in st, holding cardboard in back of work, wind yarn around 1″ width of cardboard, then pass yarn over hook, draw loop through st, yarn over and draw through 2 loops on hook (1 loop st made). Where increases are made, work 2 loop sts in same st. Slide cardboard as you work, and remove at end of round. In this pattern, loop stitch is worked *every* row, an exception to the loop stitch directions on pages 5–6.

HEAD FRONT: Starting at center, ch 6.
Rnd 1: Work 3 sc in 2nd ch from hook, sc in each of next 3 ch, 3 sc in last ch. Working along opposite edge of starting ch, sc in each of next 3 ch (12 sc). Join with sl st in first sc.
Rnd 2: Ch 1, work 2 loop sts in same st as sl st and in each st around (24 loop sts). Join with sl st in first loop st.
Rnds 3 & 4: Ch 1, work 1 loop st in same st as sl st, work 1 loop st in each st around. Join as before.
NOTE: End each rnd with sl st in first st of rnd. Start each rnd with ch 1 and work first loop st of each rnd in same st as sl st throughout.
Rnd 5: * Work 1 loop st in each of the next 3 sts, work 2 loop sts in next st. Repeat from * around (30 loop sts).
Rnd 6: Work even in loop st.
Rnd 7: * Work 1 loop st in each of the next 4 sts, work 2 loop sts in next st (increase made). Repeat from * around (36 loop sts).
Rnd 8: Working in loop st, increase one st in every 6th st (42 loop sts).
Rnd 9: Work even in loop st.
Rnd 10: Working in loop st, increase one st in every 7th st.
Rnd 11: Working in loop st, increase one st in every 8th st (54 loop sts).
Rnd 12: Work even in loop st. Break off.

HEAD BACK: Work same as head front to end of Rnd 3.
Rnds 4–8: Working in loop st, increase 6 loop sts evenly spaced on each rnd; do not increase over previous increases (54 loop sts).
Rnd 9: Work even in loop st. Break off.
To join, with right sides facing, sew both pieces of head together leaving an opening. Turn to right side. Stuff firmly and sew opening closed.

EARS: Make 2. Work same as for head front until end of Rnd 5 (30 loop sts).
Rnds 6 & 7: Work even in loop st.
Rnd 8: * Work 1 loop st in each of next 3 sts, skip next st. Repeat from * around (23 loop sts).

Rnd 9: Work even in loop st. Break off.
Fold each ear in half, stuff lightly and sew to head. Sew eyes to face. Using black yarn and tapestry needle, embroider nose in satin stitch.

BODY: Starting at neck edge, work same as for head front to end of Rnd 7.
Rnd 8: Work even in loop st (36 loop sts).
Rnd 9: Working in loop st, increase one st in every 6th st (42 loop sts).
Rnds 10–13: Work even in loop st.
Rnd 14: Working in loop st, increase one st in every 10th st (46 loop sts).
Work even on 46 loop sts until body measures 8″ from beginning. Decrease as follows:
Rnd 1: * Work 1 loop st in each of next 10 sts, skip next st. Repeat from * around.
Rnd 2: Work even on 42 loop sts.
Rnd 3: * Work 1 loop st in each of next 9 sts, skip next st. Repeat from * around (38 loop sts).
Rnds 4–7: Work even in loop st. Stuff body firmly.
Rnds 8–12: Working in loop st, decrease 6 sts evenly spaced on each rnd, adding more stuffing as you work. Break off. Sew opening closed. Sew head securely to body.

ARMS: Make 2. Starting at paw edge, ch 2.
Rnd 1: Work 6 sc in 2nd ch from hook.
Rnd 2: Work 2 sc in each sc around (12 sc).
Rnds 3 & 4: Sc in each sc around (12 sc).
Rnd 5: * Draw up loop in each of next 2 sc, yarn over and draw through all loops on hook (1 st decreased), sc in next sc. Repeat from * around.
Rnd 6: Sc in each sc around (8 sc). Join with sl st in next sc, ch 1, turn (this turn reverses direction of work).
Rnd 7: Working in loop st, * work 1 loop st in next st, work 2 loop sts in next st. Repeat from * around. Join with sl st in first loop st.
Rnd 8: Ch 1, loop st in same st as sl st, loop st in each st around (12 loop sts). Join as before. Work even in loop st for 13 more rnds. Break off. Stuff arm and sew last rnd to body.

LEGS: Make 2. Work same as for head front to end of Rnd 3 (24 loop sts).
Rnd 4: * Work 1 loop st in each of next 3 sts, skip next st. Repeat from * around.
Rnd 5: * Work 1 loop st in each of next 2 sts, skip next st. Repeat from * around. Join. Work even on 12 loop sts for 8 more rnds.
Next Rnd: * Work 2 loop sts in next st, work 1 loop st in each of next 2 sts. Repeat from * around (16 loop sts).
Next 2 Rnds: Working in loop st, increase 4 loop sts evenly spaced on each rnd.
Next Rnd: Work even in loop st (24 loop sts).
Next 3 Rnds: Continue in loop st; increase 4 loop sts evenly spaced on 1st and 3rd rnds.
Next 3 Rnds: Work even on 32 loop sts. Break off. Stuff firmly and sew last rnd to body.

FINISHING: Tie ribbon around bear's neck in a bow.

Shown in color on the back cover

GOLDILOCKS AND THE THREE BEARS

GOLDILOCKS

SIZE: About 7½″ tall.

MATERIALS: For Doll: One (20 gram—⅔ ounce) ball of tan mohair; small amount of black mohair; aluminum crochet hook size E; polyester fiberfill stuffing; tapestry needle; two ¼″ paste-on movable eyes; scrap of red felt; white glue. **For Clothes:** *J. & P. Coats Knit-Cro-Sheen*, one (175 yard) ball each of blue and white; steel crochet hook size 2; *DMC Pearl Cotton No. 3*, two (16.4 yard) skeins of yellow for hair; sewing needle.

GAUGE: For Doll: 4 sc = 1″. **For Clothes:** 6 sc = 1″. To save time, take time to check gauge.

2 JOINED DC: (Yo hook, insert hook in next st, yo hook and draw loop through, yo hook and draw through 2 loops) twice, yo hook and draw through all loops on hook.

DOLL: With tan mohair, ch 6 for top of head.
Row 1: Sc in 2nd ch from hook and each remaining ch (5 sc). Ch 1, turn.
Rows 2 & 3: 2 sc in first sc, sc in each sc across. Ch 1, turn.
Rows 4–7: Sc in each sc across (7 sc). Ch 1, turn.
Rows 8 & 9: Decrease 1 sc over first 2 sc, sc in each sc across. Ch 1, turn.
Row 10: Decrease 1 sc over first 2 sc, sc in each sc to last 2 sc, decrease 1 sc over last 2 sc (3 sc). Ch 1, turn.
Rows 11 & 12: Work even on 3 sc.
Row 13: With a separate length of tan, ch 8. Join to other end of row. Break off. Ch 9, turn. For arm, work 8 sc on chain, 3 sc on neck and 8 sc on other chain (19 sc). Ch 1, turn.
Rows 14 & 15: Work even on 19 sc. At end of Row 15, break off, turn.
  Work even on center 7 sc for 3 rows.
Next Row: Decrease 1 sc at beginning and end of row (5 sc).
Next Row: Increase 1 sc at beginning and end of row (7 sc).
Next Row: Work even on 7 sc, ch 1, turn.
For First Leg: Sc in each of next 3 sc, ch 1 turn. Work even on these 3 sc for 8 more rows. Break off tan, join black. Work even in sc for 2 rows with black. Break off.
For Second Leg: Skip 1 sc on last row of body, with tan, sc in each of last 3 sc, ch 1, turn. Complete as for first leg.
  Crochet another body piece in same manner. Sew both body pieces together, stuffing as you sew.

FINISHING: Hair: Cut pearl cotton into 9″ lengths. Arrange all lengths into an even bundle; center and drape bundle from side to side over top of head. Sew bundle to center of head forming the "part." Divide each half into three sections and braid. Tie at ends to secure, then trim ends evenly. **Face:** Glue movable eyes to face as shown in photograph. For mouth, cut a tiny oval from red felt and glue in place.

DRESS: Use blue and size 2 crochet hook.
Top: Starting at waistband, ch 31.
Row 1: Sc in 2nd ch from hook and in each remaining ch. Ch 1, turn (30 sc). Work even in sc for 4 more rows.
Row 6: Sc in each of first 6 sc for half of back, ch 1, turn. Work even on these 6 sc for 7 more rows. Break off.
Front: Skip 3 sc on last long row, sc in each of next 12 sc. Ch 1, turn. Work even on these 12 sc for 4 more rows.
Neck Opening: Work even on first 3 sc for 3 rows. Break off. Skip center 6 sc, work even on last 3 sc for 3 rows. Break off. For other half of back, skip 3 sc on last long row worked, sc in remaining 6 sc for 8 rows. Break off. Sew shoulder seams.
Skirt: Rnd 1: Make a loop on hook with blue. Working along opposite edge of starting chain of top, work * 2 dc in next st, 1 dc in next st. Repeat from * across. Ch 3, turn.
Row 2: Dc in each dc across. Ch 3, turn. Repeat last row 4 more times.
Row 7: * Sc in each of next 3 sts, ch 3, sl st in 3rd ch for picot. Repeat from * across. Break off.
Sleeves: Make 2. Starting at lower edge, ch 17.
Row 1: Work even on 16 sc for 1 row. Ch 3, turn.
Row 2: Work 2 dc in each st across. Ch 1, turn.
Row 3: Sl st in each of first 3 sts, ch 3, dc in each dc across to last 3 sts (do not work last 3 sts). Ch 3, turn.
Row 4: * Work a 2 joined dc over next 2 dc. Repeat from * across. Ch 1, turn.
Row 5: Sc in first st, * skip 1 st, sc in next st. Repeat from * across. Break off.
  Sew first 2 rows together for underarm seam. Sew sleeves into armholes. Place dress on doll with opening at back. Sew back seam.

APRON: Use white and size 2 crochet hook.
Bib Top: Starting at lower edge, ch 7.
Rows 1–3: Work even on 6 sc.
Row 4: 2 sc in first sc, sc in each sc across to last sc, 2 sc in last sc.
Rows 5 & 6: Work even on 8 sc. At end of Row 6, ch 3, turn.
First Strap: Row 1: Dc in first sc. Ch 3, turn.

Row 2: Dc in 3rd ch from hook. Ch 3, turn. Repeat Row 2 for 8 more rows, omitting last ch-3 on last row. Break off.
Second Strap: Skip center sts on last 8 sc row, join yarn in last st, ch 3, dc in same st, ch 3, turn. Complete as for first strap (10 rows in all).
Waistband and Skirt: Row 1: Ch 30, then working along opposite edge of starting chain of bib, sc in each of 6 sts, then ch 30. Break off, turn.
Row 2: Make loop on hook. Work 2 dc in each of 6 sc on Row 1. Ch 3, turn.
Rows 3–5: Dc in first dc, dc in each st across. Ch 3, turn. At end of last row, omit ch-3 and break off.
Ruffle: Make loop on hook and start at end of right strap. In each of next 10 rows of strap, work (dc, ch 1) 3 times. Continue ruffle along side edge of bib and skirt, lower edge of skirt and other edge of skirt, bib and left strap. Work (dc, ch 1) closely so work will ruffle. Break off.

Place apron on doll over dress. Tie ends of waistband at back in a bow. Cross straps in back and sew to waistband.

MAMA AND PAPA BEARS

SIZE: About 7½″ tall, standing.

MATERIALS: One (40 gram—1½ ounce) ball of brushed mohair in brown for each bear, a small amount of tan mohair; aluminum crochet hook size E; polyester fiberfill stuffing; tapestry needle; two sew-on movable eyes for each bear; one small black button for nose for each bear; 12″ piece of ⅜″-wide blue ribbon for Papa's tie; small piece of red dotted fabric for Mama's apron; small piece of ⅛″-wide ribbon for Mama's bow; a miniature broom.

GAUGE: 7 sc = 2″. To save time, take time to check gauge.

HEAD: With brown, ch 2.
Rnd 1: Work 7 sc in first ch made. Do not join rnds. Use a marker. Move marker each rnd.
Rnd 2: * 2 sc in next sc. Repeat from * around (14 sc).
Rnd 3: * 2 sc in next sc, sc in next sc. Repeat from * around (21 sc).
Rnd 4: * 2 sc in next sc, sc in each of next 2 sc. Repeat from * around (28 sc). Join with sl st to first sc of rnd. Do not break off.
For First Ear: Ch 1.
Row 1: Sc in each of next 4 sc. Ch 1, turn.
Row 2: Sc in each of the 4 sc. Ch 1, turn.
Row 3: (Decrease 1 sc over next 2 sc) twice. Break off. Skip 3 sc on head. Attach yarn in next sc and work another ear in same manner.

Make another head piece in same manner. To join, hold both head pieces together. Overcast from right side, leaving a small opening. Stuff head and ears firmly. Sew opening closed.

SNOUT: With tan, ch 2.
Rnd 1: Work 5 sc in first ch made. Do not join rnd.
Rnd 2: Work 2 sc in each sc around. Join with sl st to first sc of rnd. Break off, leaving an 8″ end. Thread end into

tapestry needle and sew snout to head, stuffing lightly. Sew black button to center of snout. Sew eyes to head above snout.

BODY: Work as for head through Rnd 4. Do not join rnd.
Rnd 5: Sc in each sc around. Join with a sl st to first sc of rnd. Make another piece in same manner.

To join, hold both body pieces together. Overcast from right side, leaving a small opening. Stuff body firmly and sew opening closed.

LEGS: Make 2. With brown, ch 8.
Row 1: Sc in 2nd ch from hook and in each remaining ch (7 sc). Ch 1, turn.
Rows 2–7: Sc in each sc. Ch 1, turn. At end of Row 7, break off. Fold first row to last row and overcast to form tube. Stuff legs and sew one end of each to body. Leave other end open until foot pads are attached.

ARMS: Make 2. With brown, ch 10.
Row 1: Sc in 2nd ch from hook and in each remaining ch (9 sc). Ch 1, turn.
Rows 2–5: Sc in each sc. Ch 1, turn. At end of Row 5, break off. Finish as for legs, sewing one end of each to body. Leave other end open until paw pads are attached.

FOOT PADS: Make 2. With tan, ch 2.
Work 9 sc in first ch made. Join with sl st to first sc. Break off, leaving an 8″ end. Thread end into tapestry needle and sew one to lower edge of each leg.

PAW PADS: Make 2. With tan, ch 2. Work 7 sc into first ch made. Finish as for foot pads and sew one to end of each arm.

FINISHING: Sew head to body. **For Papa: Tie:** Cut ends of blue ribbon to form points. Tie around neck in a Windsor knot (as for a man's tie). **For Mama: Apron:** With pinking shears (or use plain scissors), cut a U-shaped apron in center of red dotted fabric leaving a long strip at each end for ties; see photograph. Place apron on Mama and tie in back. Holding broom 1″ from end of arm, fold arm over broomstick and sew securely. Make bow from narrow red ribbon and sew to top of head.

BABY BEAR

SIZE: About 6″ tall, standing.

MATERIALS: One (20 gram—⅔ ounce) ball of brushed mohair in brown, a small amount of tan mohair; aluminum crochet hook size E; polyester fiberfill stuffing; tapestry needle; two sew-on movable eyes; one small black button for nose; 10″ piece of narrow striped ribbon for tie.

GAUGE: 7 sc = 2″. To save time, take time to check gauge.

HEAD: With brown, ch 2.

Rnd 1: Work 7 sc in first ch made. Do not join rnds. Use a marker. Move marker each rnd.

Rnd 2: * 2 sc in next sc. Repeat from * around (14 sc).

Rnd 3: * 2 sc in next sc, sc in next sc. Repeat from * around (21 sc). Join with sl st to first sc of rnd. Do not break off.

For First Ear: Ch 1.

Row 1: Sc in each of next 3 sc. Ch 1, turn.

Row 2: Sc in each of the 3 sc. Break off. Skip 3 sc on head. Attach yarn in next sc and work another ear in same manner. Make another head piece in same manner.

To join, hold both head pieces together. Overcast from right side, leaving a small opening. Stuff head and ears firmly and sew opening closed.

SNOUT: With tan, ch 2.

Rnd 1: Work 4 sc in first ch made. Do not join rnd.

Rnd 2: Work 2 sc in each sc around. Join with sl st to first sc of rnd. Break off, leaving an 8″ end. Thread end into tapestry needle and sew snout to head, stuffing lightly. Sew black button to center of snout. Sew eyes to head above snout.

BODY: Work as for head through Rnd 3. Do not join rnd.

Rnd 4: Sc in each sc around. Join with a sl st to first sc of rnd. Break off. Make another piece in same manner.

To join, hold both body pieces together. Overcast from right side, leaving a small opening. Stuff body firmly and sew opening closed.

LEGS: Make 2. With brown, ch 6.

Row 1: Sc in 2nd ch from hook and in each remaining ch (5 sc). Ch 1, turn.

Rows 2–5: Sc in each sc. Ch 1, turn. At end of Row 5, break off. Fold first row to last row and overcast to form tube. Stuff legs and sew one end of each to body. Leave other end open until foot pads are attached.

ARMS: Make 2. With brown, ch 8.

Row 1: Sc in 2nd ch from hook and in each remaining ch (7 sc). Ch 1, turn.

Rows 2–5: Sc in each sc. Ch 1, turn. At end of Row 5, break off. Finish as for legs, sewing one end of each to body. Leave other end open until paw pads are attached.

FOOT PADS: Make 2. With tan, ch 2. Work 7 sc in first ch made. Join with sl st to first sc. Break off, leaving an 8″ end. Thread end into needle and sew one to lower edge of each leg.

PAW PADS: Make 2. With tan, ch 2. Work 5 sc in first ch made. Finish as for foot pads and sew one to end of each arm.

FINISHING: Sew head to body. **Tie:** Cut ends of ribbon at a slant. Place around neck, cross ends and sew tie in front.

Shown in color on the inside back cover.

PREPPY BEAR

SIZE: About 10″ high, sitting.

MATERIALS: For Bear: *Brunswick Eleganza* (brushed mohair and acrylic sport-weight yarn), 2 (50 gram—1.75 ounce) balls of sandalwood; aluminum crochet hook size D; polyester fiberfill stuffing; tapestry needle; two 15mm animal eyes; small amount of brown mohair; brown felt; brown sewing thread; sewing needle. **For Clothes:** 1 ounce each of red and white knitting worsted; aluminum crochet hook size F.

GAUGE: For Bear: 4 sc = 1″; 5 rows = 1″. **For Clothes:** 4 sc or dc = 1″. To save time, take time to check gauge.

BEAR

BODY: Make 2. Starting at neck edge, ch 14.
Row 1: Sc in 2nd ch from hook and in each remaining ch (13 sc). Ch 1, turn.
Row 2: 2 sc in first sc, sc in each remaining sc across (14 sc). Ch 1, turn. Repeat Row 2, 9 times more.
Rows 12–23: Work even in sc on 23 sts.
Row 24: Decrease 1 sc over first 2 sc, sc in each sc to last 2 sc, decrease 1 sc over last 2 sc. Ch 1, turn.
Row 25: Sc in each sc across. Ch 1, turn. Repeat Rows 24 and 25, 3 times more.
Rows 32 & 33: (Decrease 1 sc over next 2 sc) twice, sc in each sc across to last 4 sc, (decrease 1 sc over next 2 sc) twice. Ch 1, turn. At end of Row 33, break off.

To join, hold both body pieces together with right sides facing. Leaving body open at neck edges, sc both pieces together. Turn to right side, stuff body firmly.

HEAD SIDE: Starting at neck edge, ch 13.
Row 1: Sc in 2nd ch from hook and in each remaining ch across (12 sc). Ch 1, turn.
Rows 2, 4 & 6: 2 sc in first sc, sc in each sc across, 2 sc in last sc. Ch 1, turn.
Rows 3, 5 & 7: Sc in each sc across. Ch 1, turn. At end of Row 7, mark last sc worked for nose end of piece (the next increases made are at marked edge).
Rows 8, 10 & 12: 2 sc in first sc, sc in each sc across. Ch 1, turn.
Rows 9, 11 & 13: Sc in each sc across. Ch 1, turn. At end of Row 13, do not ch 1. Turn.
Row 14: Sl st across first 6 sts, ch 1, sc in each of next 15 sc. Ch 1, turn.
Row 15: Sc in each of the next 15 sc. Ch 1, turn.
Row 16: Decrease 1 sc over first 2 sc, sc in each sc across. Ch 1, turn.
Rows 17, 18 & 19: Decrease 1 sc over first 2 sc, sc in each

sc to last 2 sc, decrease 1 sc over last 2 sc. Ch 1, turn.
Row 20: (Decrease 1 sc over next 2 sc) twice, sc in each sc across. Break off. Make another piece in same manner.

HEAD GUSSET: Starting at neck edge, ch 2.
Row 1: In first ch made, work 1 sc. Ch 1, turn.
Row 2: Work 3 sc in sc. Ch 1, turn.
Row 3: 2 sc in first sc, sc in next sc, 2 sc in last sc. Ch 1, turn.
Rows 4–6: 2 sc in first sc, sc in each sc to last sc, 2 sc in last sc. Ch 1, turn.
Row 7: Sc in each sc. Ch 1, turn.
Row 8: Repeat Row 3.
Rows 9–19: Repeat Row 7.
Row 20: Decrease 1 sc over first 2 sc, sc in each sc to last 2 sc, decrease 1 sc over last 2 sc. Ch 1, turn.
Rows 21 & 22: Sc in each sc across. Ch 1, turn. Repeat Rows 20–22, 3 times more.
Rows 32–35: Sc in each sc across. Ch 1, turn. Break off.

To join the pieces, follow the *Head Joining Diagram.* Starting at A, join the two side pieces to the head gusset matching points B and C respectively for the back of the head. Then, fold the gusset in half at D and sew the head front edges together matching points A and E. Using brown mohair, embroider a square nose in satin stitch and a mouth in fly stitch before stuffing head. Sew eyes in place (or secure eyes if using other than sew-on eyes). Stuff head firmly and sew to body, matching body seams to center front and back of head.

EARS: Make 4. Starting at lower edge, ch 11.
Row 1: Sc in 2nd ch from hook and in each remaining ch (10 sc). Ch 1, turn.
Rows 2–5: Decrease 1 sc over first 2 sc, sc in each sc across. Ch 1, turn.
Row 6: Decrease 1 sc over first 2 sc, sc in each sc across to last 2 sc, decrease 1 sc over last 2 sc. Break off. Secure two ear pieces together with an overcast stitch for each ear. Stuff lightly and sew to sides of head as shown in photograph.

ARMS: Make 4. Starting at top edge, ch 9. Work even on 8 sc for 9 rows.
Rows 11 & 12: Decrease 1 sc over first 2 sc, sc in each sc to last 2 sc, decrease 1 sc over last 2 sc. Ch 1, turn.
Row 13: 3 sc in first sc, sc in each sc across, 3 sc in last sc (8 sc). Ch 1, turn. Work even on 8 sc for 3 more rows.
Rows 17 & 18: Repeat Rows 11 and 12. Break off.
Leaving top edge open, join 2 pieces together for each arm with an overcast stitch. Stuff arms and sew to body.

Using paw pattern, cut 2 pieces from brown felt. Sew in place with brown sewing thread.

LEGS: Make 4. Starting at top edge, ch 10.
Row 1: Sc in 2nd ch from hook and in each remaining ch (9 sc). Ch 1, turn.
Work even on 9 sc for 12 rows. At end of Row 12, ch 5, turn.
Row 13: Sc in 2nd ch from hook and in each of remaining 3 ch, sc in each sc (13 sc). Ch 1, turn.
Row 14: Sc in each sc across. Ch 1, turn.
Rows 15 & 16: Decrease 1 sc over first 2 sc, sc in each sc to last 2 sc, decrease 1 sc over last 2 sc. Break off.

FOOT PADS: Make 2. Ch 6.
Rnd 1: Work 5 sc in 2nd ch from hook, work 1 sc in each of next 3 ch, then work 5 sc in last ch; working along opposite edge of ch, work 1 sc in each of next 3 sts. Join with sl st. Ch 1.
Rnd 2: 2 sc in each of next 5 sc, sc in each of next 3 sc, 2 sc in each of next 5 sc, sc in each of next 3 sc. Join and break off. Using crocheted foot pads for pattern, cut 2 oval foot pads from brown felt.

Join 2 pieces for each leg, inserting crocheted foot pad at lower edge and leaving top edge open. With brown sewing thread, sew felt foot pads in place. Stuff and sew legs to sides of body as shown in photograph.

SWEATER

BACK: Starting at lower edge, with red, ch 30.
Row 1: Work 1 dc in 4th ch from hook and in each remaining ch (28 dc, counting starting ch as 1 dc). Ch 1, turn.
Row 2 (right side): Sc in each dc across, sc in top of turning ch. Attach white, drop red, turn.
Row 3: With white, ch 3, skip first sc, dc in each remaining sc across. Ch 1, turn.
Row 4 (decrease row): Working in sc, decrease 1 sc over first 2 dc, sc in each dc across to last 2 dc, decrease 1 sc over last 2 dc (26 sc). Break off white, pick up red, turn.

Row 5: With red, ch 3, skip first dc, dc in each remaining sc across (26 dc). Turn.
Row 6: For armholes, sl st in each of first 4 dc, ch 1, sc in each of next 18 dc, do not work in last 4 dc. Drop red. Turn.
Row 7: Attach white and ch 3, skip first sc, dc in each remaining sc across (18 dc). Ch 1, turn.
Row 8: Sc in each dc across. Break off white.
Rows 9 & 10: With red, repeat Rows 7 & 8 (18 sts).
Row 11 (neckband): Turn work. Skip 2 sc for shoulder, attach white and sc in each of next 14 sc. Do not work last 2 sc for other shoulder. Ch 1, turn.
Row 12: Sc in each sc across. Break off.

FRONT: Work same as for back.

FINISHING: Sew shoulder seams together leaving neck-band seams and side seams open. With red, work 1 row of sc across each armhole. Put sweater on bear, and sew neckband seams, then weave side seams from lower edge to beginning of armholes using matching thread.

CAP

Starting at center, with red, ch 2.
Rnd 1: Work 8 sc in 2nd ch from hook. Work in back loops of sc throughout, except on brim.
Rnd 2: Work 2 sc in each sc around (16 sc).
Rnd 3: * 2 sc in next sc, sc in next sc. Repeat from * around (24 sc).
Rnd 4: * 2 sc in next sc, sc in each of next 2 sc. Repeat from * around (32 sc).
Rnd 5: Sc in each sc around.
Rnd 6: * 2 sc in next sc, sc in each of next 3 sc. Repeat from * around (40 sc).
Rnd 7: Sc in each sc around; turn.
Brim Row 1: Decrease 1 sc over first 2 sc, sc in each of next 5 sc, decrease 1 sc over next 2 sc. Ch 1, turn.
Row 2: Decrease 1 sc over first 2 sc, sc in each of next 3 sc, decrease 1 sc over last 2 sc. Break off.

Work 1 row of sl st loosely around brim. Stuff cap lightly and sew to head.

PREPPY BEAR PATTERNS

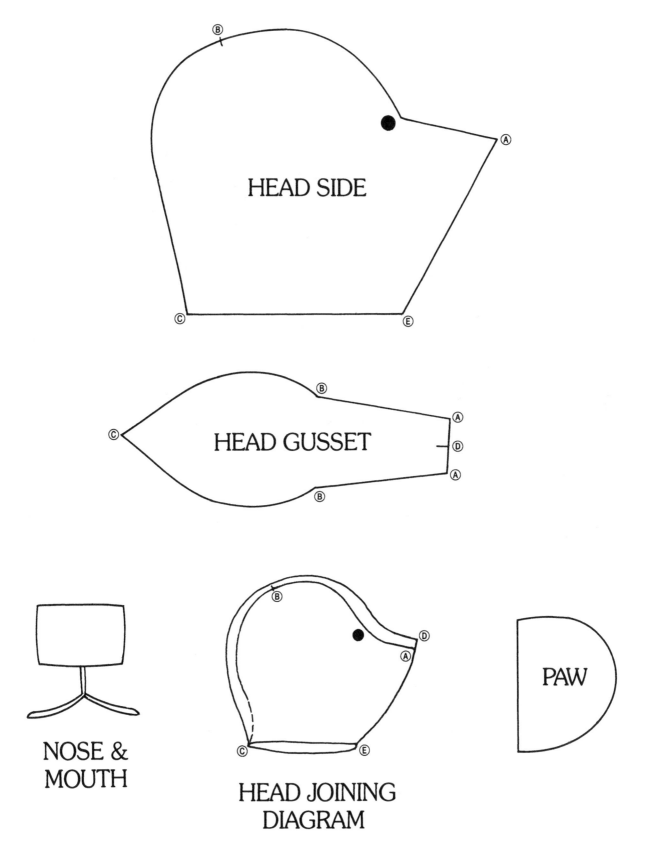

HEAD SIDE

HEAD GUSSET

NOSE &
MOUTH

HEAD JOINING
DIAGRAM

PAW

Shown in color on the front cover.

HONEY BEAR

SIZE: About 10″ high, sitting.

MATERIALS: For Bear: 3½ ounces of golden brown chenille yarn; aluminum crochet hook size H; polyester fiberfill stuffing; tapestry needle; two 16mm sew-on animal eyes; black sew-on plastic nose. **For Honey Hive:** 1 ounce of light gold bulky yarn; aluminum crochet hook size I; polyester fiberfill stuffing; tapestry needle; several yards of black yarn for embroidery. **For T Shirt:** ½ yard of red cotton knit fabric; red sewing thread; 2 snap fasteners.

GAUGE: 8 sc = 3″. To save time, take time to check gauge.

BODY: Starting at lower edge with chenille, ch 2.
Rnd 1: Work 8 sc in first ch made. Do not join rnds. Use a marker, move marker each rnd.
Rnd 2: Work 2 sc in each sc around (16 sc).
Rnd 3: * Work 2 sc in next sc, sc in next sc. Repeat from * around (24 sc).
Rnd 4: * Work 2 sc in next sc, sc in each of next 2 sc. Repeat from * around (32 sc).
Rnd 5: * Work 2 sc in next sc, sc in each of next 3 sc. Repeat from * around (40 sc).
Work even on 40 sc for 5″ more. Stuff body firmly.
Decrease Rnds 1 & 2: * Decrease 1 sc over next 2 sc. Repeat from * around. Break off. Add more stuffing. Leave top edge open for neck.

HEAD: With chenille, ch 2.
Rnd 1: Work 5 sc in first ch made.
Rnds 2 & 3: Work 2 sc in each sc around.
Rnd 4: Sc in each sc around (20 sc).
Rnd 5: * Work 2 sc in next sc, sc in next sc. Repeat from * around (30 sc).
Rnd 6: * Work 1 sc in each of next 2 sc, 2 sc in next sc. Repeat from * around (40 sc).
Rnd 7: Sc in each sc around. Break off.
Make another piece in same manner. Sew or crochet both head pieces together, leaving an opening. Stuff firmly, then sew opening closed. Sew head securely to body.

SNOUT: With chenille, ch 2.
Rnd 1: Work 4 sc in first ch made.
Rnd 2: (Work 2 sc in next sc, 1 sc in next sc) twice.
Rnds 3 & 4: Work 2 sc in each sc around.
Rnd 5: Work 1 sc in each sc around. Break off. Stuff and sew snout to lower portion of face as shown in photograph.

EARS: Make 4. With chenille, ch 7.
Row 1: Work 1 sc in 2nd ch from hook and in each remaining ch (6 sc). Ch 1, turn.
Rows 2 & 3: Decrease 1 sc over first 2 sc, sc in each remaining sc. Break off.
Sew or crochet two pieces together to form each ear. Sew ears to head as shown in photograph.

ARMS/LEGS: Make 4. With chenille, ch 2.
Rnd 1: Work 8 sc in first ch made.

Rnd 2: Work 2 sc in each sc around (16 sc).
Work even on 16 sc until piece measures 4″ from beginning. Break off.
Stuff until firm, then sew arms and legs to body as shown in photograph.

FINISHING: Sew eyes and nose to face.

T-SHIRT

Trace complete pattern for Honey Bear's collar and quarter-pattern for shirt; trace quarter-pattern in reverse along dot/dash line to make a half pattern. Use patterns to cut 1 shirt and 2 collars from red fabric, placing patterns on fold of fabric where indicated. Stitch all pieces together with right sides facing and raw edges even, making ¼″ seams; press all seam allowances open unless otherwise directed.

Slash shirt along foldline for center back; turn raw edges ¼″ to wrong side and stitch in place. Sew side/underarm seams of shirt; clip seam allowances to stitching line at underarms. Make a ½″ hem at edge of each sleeve and at bottom edge of shirt; topstitch in place.

Fold each collar piece as indicated; stitch center back edges. Turn to right side and press; stitch remaining raw edges together ⅛″ from edges. Pin raw edge of one collar piece to neckline of shirt, matching notch on collar to center front of shirt; match back of collar to opening at shirt back. Pin raw edge of second collar to other edge of neckline in same manner; pieces will overlap at center front. Stitch; press seam allowance toward shirt and topstitch in place. Sew snaps along back edge of shirt.

HONEY HIVE

Top Section: With light gold, ch 2.
Rnd 1: Work 5 sc in first ch made.
Rnd 2: Work 2 sc in each sc around (10 sc).
Rnd 3: * Work 2 sc in next sc, sc in next sc. Repeat from * around (15 sc).
Rnd 4: * Work 2 sc in next sc, sc in each of next 2 sc. Repeat from * around (20 sc).
Rnd 5: * Work 2 sc in next sc, sc in each of next 3 sc. Repeat from * around (25 sc).
Rnd 6: * Work 2 sc in next sc, sc in each of next 4 sc. Repeat from * around (30 sc).
Work even on 30 sc for 6 rnds more. Break off.
Bottom: With light gold, ch 2.
Rnd 1: Work 8 sc in first ch made.
Rnd 2: Work 2 sc in each sc around (16 sc).
Rnds 3 & 4: Work in sc, increasing 7 sc evenly spaced around.
Rnd 5: Sc in each sc around. Break off.

FINISHING: Crochet bottom piece to top piece with light gold yarn, stuffing as you work. With black yarn embroider a cross-stitch on top of hive; work overcast stitches around bottom as shown in photograph.

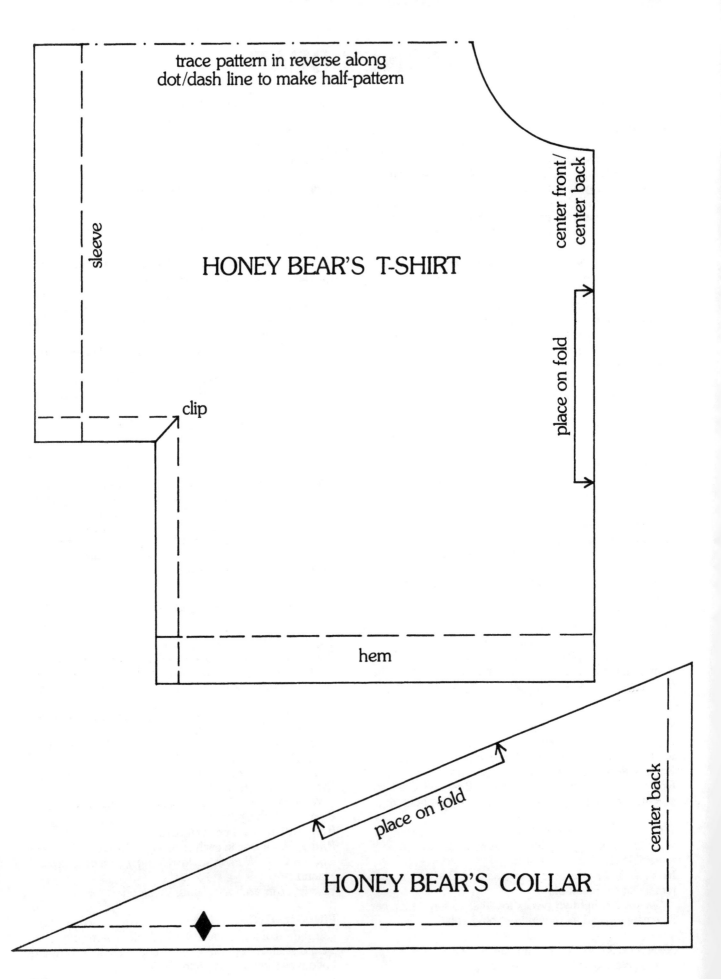

trace pattern in reverse along
dot/dash line to make half-pattern

sleeve

center front/
center back

HONEY BEAR'S T-SHIRT

place on fold

clip

hem

place on fold

center back

HONEY BEAR'S COLLAR

34

ROOSEVELT BEARS

TEDDY G—THE CLOWN

SIZE: About 13″ high, sitting.

MATERIALS: For Bear: 8 ounces of bulky-weight thick-and-thin brushed wool in tan; aluminum crochet hook size K; polyester fiberfill stuffing; tapestry needle; two 16mm sew-on animal eyes; black plastic sew-on nose; several yards of black mohair yarn for embroidery. **For Clown Costume:** ½ yard 44″-wide blue/white polka dot fabric; 5 yards 1″-wide yellow bias tape (or fabric to cut your own); narrow flat elastic; blue and yellow sewing thread; snap fasteners; three red ½″ pompons; one white 1″ pompon; small piece of double adhesive iron-on interlining.

GAUGE: 2 sc = 1″. To save time, take time to check gauge.

BEAR

BODY: With tan, starting at lower edge, ch 2.
Rnd 1: Work 7 sc in first ch made. Do not join rnds. Use a marker, move marker each rnd.
Rnd 2: Work 2 sc in each sc around (14 sc).
Rnd 3: Work 2 sc in each sc around (28 sc).
   Work even on 28 sc for 6″ more. Stuff body firmly as you work.
Decrease Rnds 1 & 2: * Decrease 1 sc over next 2 sc. Repeat from * around. Break off. Leave top edge open for neck.

HEAD FRONT: With tan, starting at tip of nose, ch 2.
Rnd 1: Work 4 sc in first ch made. Do not join rnds. Use a marker, move marker each rnd.
Rnd 2: Work 2 sc in first sc, sc in next sc, 2 sc in next sc, sc in next sc (6 sc).
Rnd 3: (Work 2 sc in next sc, sc in each of next 2 sc) twice (8 sc).
Rnd 4: Work 2 sc in next sc, sc in each of next 2 sc, 2 sc in next sc, sc in each of next 4 sc (10 sc).
Rnd 5: Work sc in next sc, 2 sc in next sc, sc in each of next 2 sc, 2 sc in next sc, sc in next sc, 2 sc in next sc, sc in each of next 2 sc, 2 sc in next sc (14 sc).
Rnd 6: Work sc in each of next 2 sc, 3 sc in next sc, sc in each of next 2 sc, 3 sc in next sc, sc in each of next 3 sc, 2 sc in next sc, sc in each of next 2 sc, 2 sc in next sc, sc in next sc (20 sc).
Rnd 7: Work sc in each of next 3 sc, 3 sc in next sc, sc in each of next 4 sc, 3 sc in next sc, sc in each of next 5 sc, 2 sc in next sc, sc in each of next 2 sc, 2 sc in next sc, sc in each of next 2 sc (26 sc).

Rnd 8: Work sc in each of next 3 sc, 3 sc in next sc, sc in each of next 8 sc, 3 sc in next sc, sc in each of next 6 sc, 2 sc in next sc, sc in each of next 2 sc, 2 sc in next sc, sc in each of next 3 sc (32 sc).
Rnd 9: * Work 2 sc in next sc, sc in each of next 3 sc. Repeat from * around (40 sc). Break off.

HEAD BACK: With tan, ch 2.
Rnd 1: Work 5 sc in first ch made.
Rnd 2: Work 2 sc in each sc around (10 sc).
Rnds 3–5: Continue to work in sc, increasing 5 sc evenly spaced on each rnd (20 sc).
Rnd 6: Continue to work in sc, increasing 7 sc evenly spaced around (27 sc).
Rnd 7: Continue to work in sc, increasing 8 sc evenly spaced around (35 sc). Break off.
   Sew or crochet head front to head back, stuffing as you work.

EARS: Make 2. With tan, ch 6 for lower edge.
Row 1: Sc in 2nd ch from hook and in each remaining ch (5 sc).
Rows 2 & 3: Decrease 1 sc over first 2 sc, sc in each remaining sc.
Row 4: Sc in each sc across (3 sc). Break off. Sew ears to head.

ARMS/LEGS: Make 4. With tan, starting at lower edge, ch 2.
Rnd 1: Work 4 sc in first ch made.
Rnd 2: Work 2 sc in each sc around (8 sc).
   Working in rnds, work even on 8 sc until piece measures 4″ from beginning. Stuff until firm, then sew arms and legs to body as shown in photograph.

FINISHING: Sew head to body. Sew eyes and nose to face. With black mohair and tapestry needle, embroider mouth in outline stitch.

CLOWN OUTFIT

Stitch all pieces together with right sides facing and raw edges even, making ¼″ seams; press all seam allowances open.

CLOWN SUIT: Trace patterns for Teddy G's sleeve and clown suit. The clown suit pattern has been divided into two pieces in order to fit full-size in this book; when tracing the pattern, connect pieces along dotted lines, matching letters. Use patterns to cut 2 sleeves and 2 clown suits from blue polka dot fabric, placing patterns on fold of fabric where indicated.

Shown in color on the inside front cover.

Slash along fold of one suit piece to notch for center back opening. Fold and press raw edges at center back ⅛" to wrong side twice; topstitch in place. Pin sleeves into armhole openings matching notches; stitch together (all pieces will now be connected). Bind raw edges at neck, sleeves and legs with yellow double fold bias tape. Make a casing for elastic along dot/dash line at neck using bias tape. Sew side/underarm seam of suit and sleeve. Sew legs of suit together along inseam, clipping at curves where necessary. From elastic, cut two 5" lengths for sleeves, two 5" lengths for legs and one 12" length for neck. Stretching as you sew and using a zigzag stitch on your sewing machine, stitch elastic to wrong side of suit along dot/dash lines on sleeves and legs. Run elastic through casing at neck; stitch at each end to secure. Sew snaps along opening at center back. Sew or glue 3 red pompons to center front of clown suit.

HAT: Trace pattern for Teddy G's clown hat. Use pattern to cut 2 pieces from blue polka dot fabric and 1 piece from double adhesive iron-on interlining. Sandwich interlining between wrong sides of blue fabric and iron following manufacturer's instructions. Sew straight seam of hat, forming a cone; turn to right side. Use 1½ yards of yellow double fold bias tape for hat trim as follows: fold bias tape in half with wrong sides facing and press; baste close to edges. Pull basting thread to gather strip to fit around bottom edge of hat; pin, then stitch in place, adjusting gathers evenly. Glue or stitch white pompon to tip of hat. Place hat on bear's head and tack in place.

TEDDY B—THE RINGMASTER

SIZE: About 19" high, standing.

MATERIALS: For Bear: 8 ounces of bulky-weight thick-and-thin brushed wool in brown; aluminum crochet hook size K; polyester fiberfill stuffing; tapestry needle; two 16mm sew-on movable eyes; black plastic sew-on nose.
For Ringmaster's Costume: ⅓ yard each of red and black satin fabric; red and black sewing thread; four snap fasteners; four buttons; one black pipe cleaner.

BEAR

With brown, work as for Teddy G. Omit embroidered mouth.

RINGMASTER'S OUTFIT

Stitch all pieces together with right sides facing and raw edges even making ¼" seams; press all seam allowances open.

COAT: Trace patterns for Teddy B's coat front, coat back, sleeve, sleeve facing, collar, front facing and back facing. Use patterns to cut the following from red satin fabric, being sure to reverse each pattern when cutting the second piece (if patterns are placed on doubled fabric, the second piece will automatically be cut in reverse); 2 coat fronts, 1 coat back, 2 sleeves, 1 back facing. Cut the following from black satin fabric in same manner: 1 collar, 2 front facings, 2 sleeve facings.

Stitch coat front pieces to coat back at shoulders. Pin sleeves into armhole openings matching notch on sleeve to shoulder seam and easing to fit; stitch together. Pin sleeve facing to end of each sleeve; stitch straight edges together. Press facing to right side of sleeve, fold raw edge ¼" to wrong side and topstitch in place with black thread. Stitch side/sleeve edges of coat matching underarm seams.

Fold collar in half and stitch short side edges; turn to right side and press. Pin collar to neck edge of coat on right side matching dots at center back and easing to fit; collar will end at center front on each side. Stitch together; clip seam allowance if necessary and press to inside of coat.

Stitch front facings to back facing at sides matching dots. Press raw inner edges ⅛" to wrong side, clipping as necessary; topstitch in place. Pin facing to coat matching raw edges, seams, notches and dots; stitch together. Clip to dot at center back; turn facing to right side and press carefully. Topstitch tails on coat back if desired. Press lapels on coat front to right side as shown in photograph.

Sew snaps to right coat front at each X. Sew snaps to left front facing to match. Sew one black button over each snap on left coat front.

PANTS: Trace patterns for Teddy B's pants and waistband. Use patterns to cut the following from black satin fabric: 2 pants, 1 waistband (placed on fold of fabric).

Stitch inseams of each pants piece together, making 2 separate legs; make ¼" hem at end of each leg. Turn one leg to right side and insert inside other leg matching crotch seam. Stitch from center front to dot at center back. Turn to right side.

Pin waistband to pants matching notches at sides; stitch. Press seam allowance toward waistband and topstitch in place. Fold raw edges at back opening ⅛" to wrong side; topstitch in place. Fold raw top edge ⅛" to wrong side twice; topstitch in place. Sew snaps along back opening at X's.

FINISHING: Shape black pipecleaner into eyeglasses and tack to face.

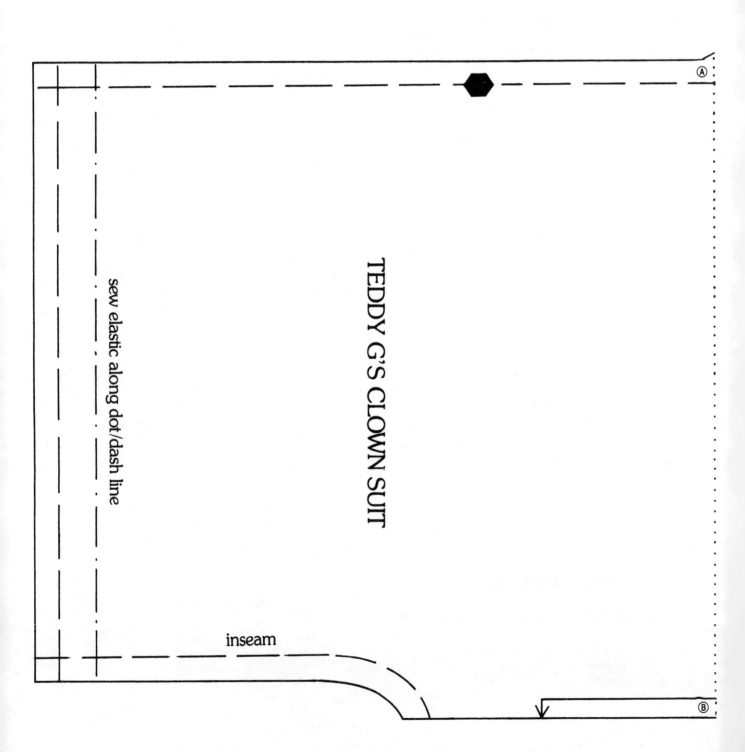

TEDDY G'S CLOWN SUIT

sew elastic along dot/dash line

inseam

Ⓐ

Ⓑ

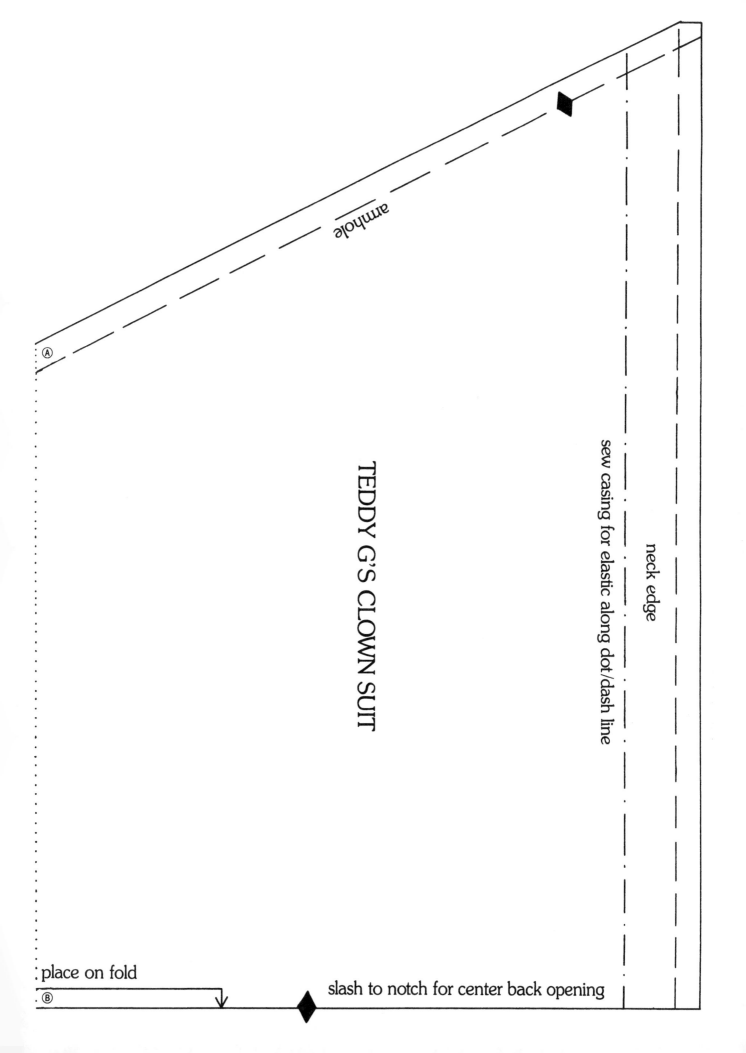

TEDDY G'S CLOWN SUIT

armhole

Ⓐ

sew casing for elastic along dot/dash line

neck edge

place on fold

Ⓑ

slash to notch for center back opening

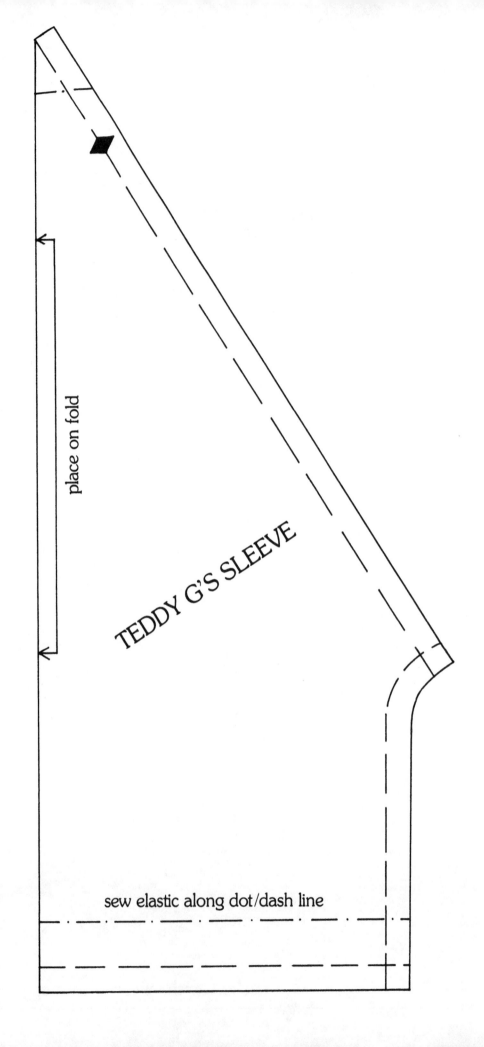

place on fold

TEDDY G'S SLEEVE

sew elastic along dot/dash line

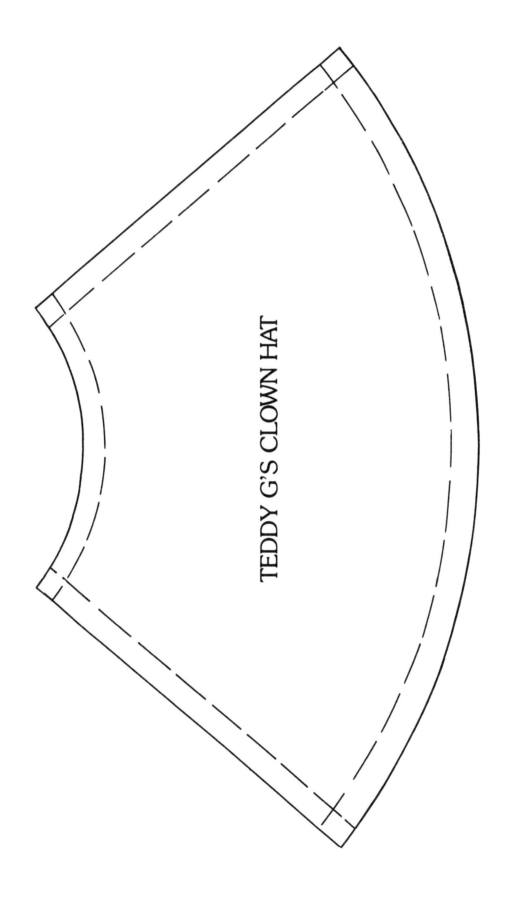

TEDDY G'S CLOWN HAT

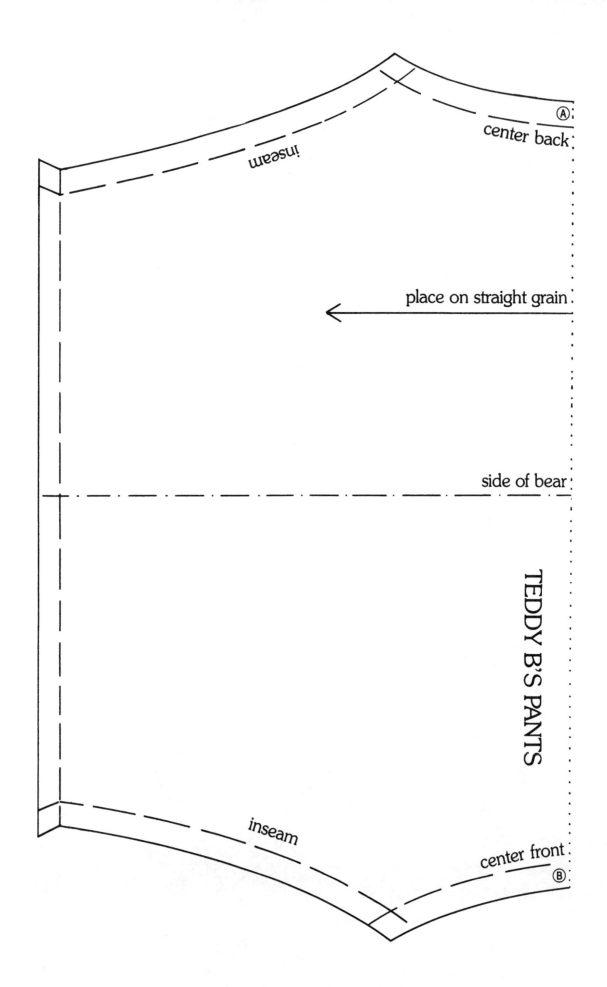

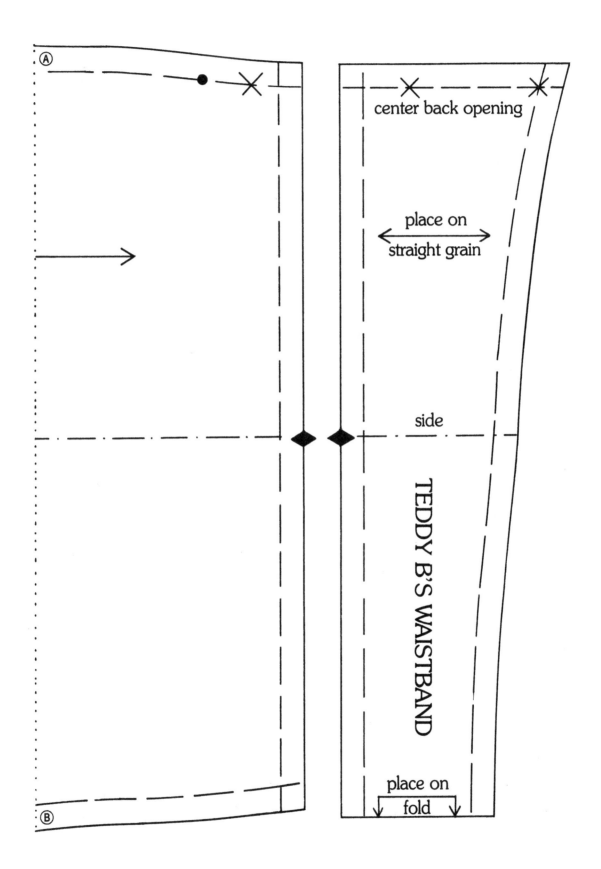

Ⓐ

center back opening

place on
straight grain

side

TEDDY B'S WAISTBAND

place on
fold

Ⓑ

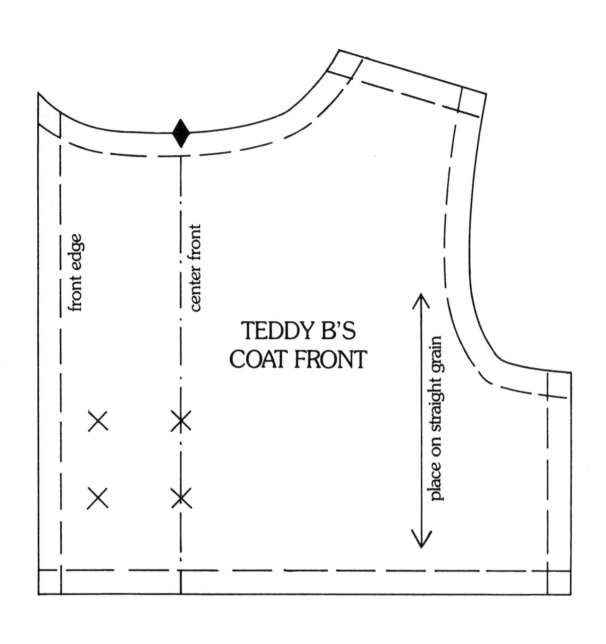

front edge

center front

TEDDY B'S
COAT FRONT

place on straight grain

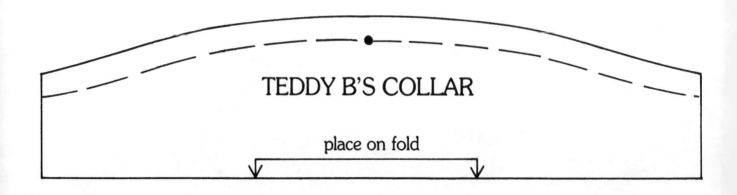

TEDDY B'S COLLAR

place on fold

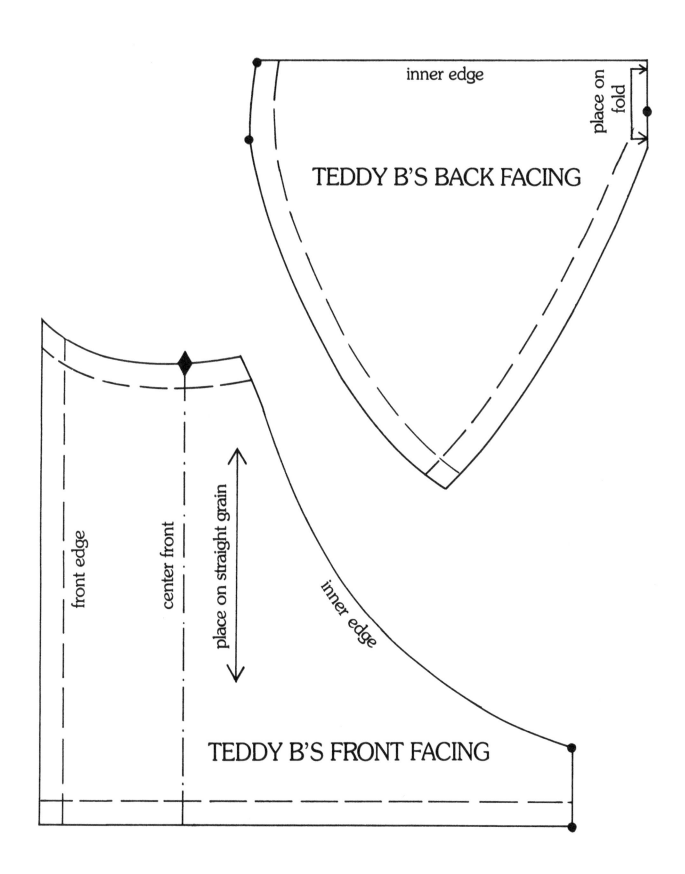

TEDDY B'S BACK FACING

inner edge

place on fold

TEDDY B'S FRONT FACING

front edge

center front

place on straight grain

inner edge

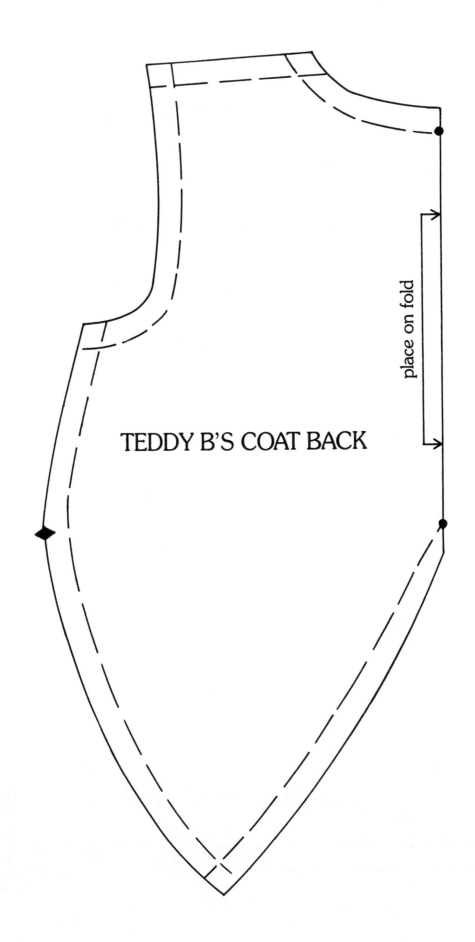

TEDDY B'S COAT BACK

place on fold

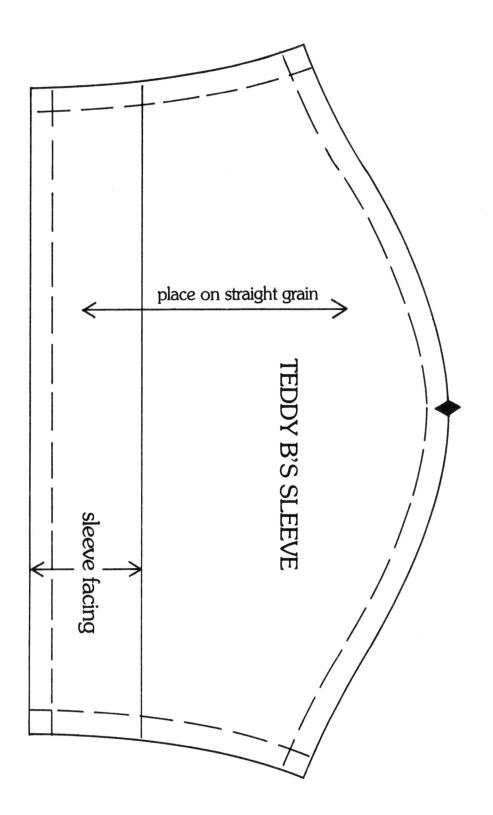

place on straight grain

TEDDY B'S SLEEVE

sleeve facing

SOURCES OF SUPPLY

Be sure to check your telephone directory first for local shops that sell these supplies; quite often, these shops will have exactly what you need or they may be able to special-order for you. In addition, a wide variety of crafts supplies can be found online.